Hedge Fund Agreements Line by Line

A User's Guide to LLC Operating Contracts

2nd EDITION

Gregory J. Nowak, Esq.

ASPATORE

Mat # 40896253

ISBN 978-0-314-90953-2

For corrections, updates, comments, or any other inquiries, please e-mail
TLR.AspatoreEditorial@thomson.com.

First Printing, 2009
10 9 8 7 6 5 4 3 2 1

ASPATORE

Aspatore Books, a Thomson Reuters business, exclusively publishes C-Level executives (CEO, CFO, CTO, CMO, Partner) from the world's most respected companies and law firms. C-Level Business Intelligence™, as conceptualized and developed by Aspatore Books, provides professionals of all levels with proven business intelligence from industry insiders—direct and unfiltered insight from those who know it best—as opposed to third-party accounts offered by unknown authors and analysts. Aspatore Books is committed to publishing an innovative line of business and legal books, those which lay forth principles and offer insights that, when employed, can have a direct financial impact on the reader's business objectives, whatever they may be. In essence, Aspatore publishes critical tools for all business professionals.

CONTENTS

Foreword

Since the publication of the first edition of *Hedge Fund Agreements Line by Line*, we have experienced the apex of the equities markets, significant financial product engineering and innovation, and the deepest economic contraction since the Great Depression. Investment banking as a separate business all but disappeared, with all of the large houses becoming associated with banks (or becoming bank holding companies themselves) to help build capital. Hedge funds participated in both the drive up and the relentless fall back down. Given their ability to profit on both the upward and downward movement of the market, most did quite well. But the volatility in the marketplace and investor demands for liquidity put impossible pressures on others, resulting in their "gating," merger, or liquidation in some cases.

While one never wants to prepare "to fight the last war," the turbulence of the financial markets during the 2007 to 2009 period, and the pressures that turbulence placed on hedge funds during that time, have provided the foundation for a complete rewrite of the ABC Fund LLC Model Agreement. As with the first edition, the commentary—the why's and how's of a particular provision—is provided in the form of reference notes. Also, as with the first edition, the Model Agreement in this second edition takes a "kitchen sink" approach and includes almost every provision on an issue. This has been done for pedagogical reasons. For this reason, the Model Agreement should not be used whole without first being modified by a lawyer with knowledge of the industry and the relevant statutes and rules that govern this area of the financial markets. This book is not intended as legal advice and cannot be relied on as such. Also, the views expressed herein are exclusively those of the author and not the publisher, Pepper Hamilton LLP or any partner or employee thereof, or any other person.

Acknowledgments

As with any endeavor of this sort, there is a host of people who have contributed in one way or other to its completion and success.

First, I would like to acknowledge the partners of Pepper Hamilton LLP for their encouragement and support—in particular, Rick Eckman, head of the Financial Services Group; Joe Del Raso, head of the Investment Management Practice Group; Steve Bortnick, of the Tax Group; and my colleagues Carol Degener, of counsel, and Matthew Silver and Janaki Catanzarite, associates in the Investment Management Group. I would also like to thank my secretary, Denise Turner, and the incredible word processors of the Pepper Support Services Group for their assistance. I would also like to acknowledge Beth M. Wiener, CPA, partner, and Barry T. Goodman, CPA, manager in the Alternative Investment Group, of the accounting firm Marcum LLP, for their assistance with FAS 157 and the American Institute of Certified Public Accountants' position with respect to valuation issues for investment companies, in general. Finally, I would like to thank my wife, Denise Nowak, and my family for their forbearance as I grappled with deadlines and time away from them to complete this manuscript.

Line-by-Line Analysis

LIMITED LIABILITY COMPANY AGREEMENT
OF
ABC FUND LLC
(A Delaware Limited Liability Company)[1]

THIS LIMITED LIABILITY COMPANY AGREEMENT is made as of July ___, 2009, by and among ABC Partners Inc., as Member Manager, and those other Persons listed from time to time on the schedule of Members maintained by the Company (the "*Schedule of Members*")[2] who shall execute this Agreement or on whose behalf this Agreement is hereafter executed,

---

[1] This limited liability company is based on the limited liability company statute of the state of Delaware. Most practitioners find that Delaware law tends to be at the cutting edge of legal practice, and hence even if the limited liability company is operated by a manager located in another state, the organic documents of the Fund are prepared under Delaware law. This also allows the Fund access to the Delaware Chancery Court, which by most accounts is the premier business court in the United States.

[2] The Operating Agreement of the ABC Fund LLC (also referred to as the "Operating Agreement" and the "Model Agreement") requires a separate Schedule of Members, rather than requiring an ongoing amendment of this document to reflect new Member admissions or withdrawals. One of the basic distinctions between documents that are "hedge Fund-centric" as opposed to "private equity Fund-centric" is the open nature of the investor roster in hedge funds as opposed to the closed nature in private equity funds. There are a variety of reasons why private equity funds tend to have a limited number of closings (valuation, capital calls, and deal flow are on the top of the list). As a matter of legal convenience, it makes sense for the manager of a hedge Fund to maintain the Schedule of Members apart for confidentiality reasons, and the list should not be an exhibit per se to the operating agreement.

whether in counterpart, by separate instrument, pursuant to power of attorney, or otherwise, as Members.[3]

WHEREAS, the Company was formed as a Limited Liability Company upon the filing of a Certificate of Formation dated as of July ___ 2009, in the office of the Secretary of State of the State of Delaware on July ___ 2009

WHEREAS, the Persons executing this Agreement desire to provide for the governance of the Company, to establish their respective rights and duties relating to the Company; and

WHEREAS, the Company is taxed as a partnership for Federal income tax purposes, meaning all income and gains and losses realized by the Company are reported by the Members as if they were partners in a limited partnership for federal and state income tax purposes.[4]

NOW THEREFORE, intending to be legally bound, in consideration of the agreements and obligations set forth herein and for other good and valuable consideration, the receipt and sufficiency of which are hereby acknowledged, the Members hereby agree as follows:

---

[3] I ordinarily recommend that the subscription agreement signed by all Members joining a Fund also contain a counterpart signature page to the limited liability company operating agreement. The Member signs only once as opposed to multiple times.

[4] Virtually all U.S.-based hedge funds elect to be taxed as a partnership for U.S. federal income tax purposes. There are collateral consequences to this election, which are discussed below, but the most notable among them are flow-through of debt-financed portfolio income for charities and pension plans that are sensitive to unrelated business taxable income for federal tax purposes, and limitations on deductions pursuant to the 2 percent floor on itemized deductions imposed by Section 67 of the Internal Revenue Code of 1986, as amended (the Code).

ARTICLE 1
DEFINITIONS[5]

1.1   Definitions. In this Agreement, the following terms shall have the meanings set forth below:

"*ABC Partners Inc.*" shall have the meaning ascribed to it in Section 2.3.

"*Account*" shall have the meaning ascribed to it in Section 5.2(a).

"*Accounting Agent*" shall mean a person appointed and for the time being acting as accounting agent of the Company as described in the Offering Memorandum.

"*Act*" shall mean the Limited Liability Company Act of the State of Delaware, Title 6, Chapter 18, 101 *et seq.* of the Delaware Code, as the same may be amended from time to time.

"*Adjusted Capital Account Deficit*" shall mean, with respect to any Member, the deficit balance, if any, in such Member's Capital Account as of the end of the relevant Performance Year, after giving effect to the following adjustments: (A) credit to such Capital Account any amounts which such Member is obligated to restore or is deemed to be obligated to restore pursuant to the penultimate sentence of Treas. Reg. §1.704-2(g)(1) and §1.704-2(i)(5); and (B) debit to such Capital Account the items described in Treas. Reg. §1.704-1(b)(2)(ii)(*d*)(4), (5) and (6). This definition of Adjusted

---

[5] A pet peeve of mine is the tendency of some draftspersons to place definitions as an endnote to an agreement or, worse, lazily ignore the convenience of the reader and bury definitions in the text. These documents are complicated enough; there is no reason to compound the problem by forcing the reader to go on a wild goose chase trying to find the defined terms. The definitions are essential to an understanding of how the Fund should operate, and therefore should be easily accessible.

Capital Account Deficit is intended to comply with the provisions of Treas. Reg. §1.704-1(b)(2)(ii)(*d*) and shall be interpreted consistently therewith.[6]

"Administrator" shall mean a person appointed and for the time being acting as administrator of the Company as described in the Offering Memorandum.[7]

"Advance" shall have the meaning ascribed to it in Section 6.11.

"Advisers Act" shall mean the Investment Advisers Act of 1940, as amended from time to time, and/or to the extent that the Member Manager or Investment Manager may be registered with one or more states, the equivalent rules and regulations applicable to state registered investment

---

[6] This is one of the first definitions and concepts of the many included in this agreement that rely on U.S. federal income tax principles. Translated, the adjusted capital account deficit is the negative balance in a Member's capital account after taking into account the Member's obligation to pay back amounts, and other adjustments required by the Treasury Regulations.

And while many are fond of denigrating Section 704 of the Internal Revenue Code and the regulations promulgated thereunder as being too complicated and unwieldy, I have yet to see a workable alternative for properly allocating gains and losses and keeping track of the relative business interests of the investors. Equalization accounting (used in many offshore funds where the law and accounting rules of the jurisdiction allow it) has its shortcomings. Another viable alternative is co-ownership of property, such as tenant-in-common arrangements. Such accounting mechanisms have a tendency to be susceptible to abuse; whereas the tried and true allocation provisions of Section 704 of the Code and the companion regulations provide a structure and discipline not present in these other arrangements. As you can surmise, the Model Agreement uses the Code's concepts as appropriate.

[7] The Model Agreement provides for both an "accounting agent" and an "administrator." In many business arrangements, one entity or person can discharge both duties. Also, as a note to the reader, this document does take a "kitchen sink" approach and includes many provisions, which, in the ordinary course of preparing Fund documents, would be identified as redundant and possibly conflicting. They are offered here for purposes of explanation and explication.

advisers in the state(s) the Member Manager or Investment Manager are registered.[8]

---

[8] During most of the time that hedge funds were growing to their current prominence, advisers were able to take advantage of certain exceptions to adviser registration under the Investor Advisers Act of 1940. Avoiding registration became an art as much as a science. This strategy came under attack in recent years. First, the marketplace began to dictate, in response to the demands of institutional investors, that the managers of hedge funds register under the Advisers Act. Second, managers have become aware of the fact that if they are just registered under state law, instead of federal law, they may very well be precluded from accepting a performance allocation. (See, e.g., Delaware law applicable to non-federally registered advisers; Delaware Securities Act Sections 7301, 7302, and 7317(b)(1).) Third, the Securities and Exchange Commission had attempted to redefine the term "client" under Advisers Act Rule 203(b)(3)-1. The rule would have required managers to look through Fund entities and count the investors in the funds for purposes of determining if the manager had more than fourteen clients and were therefore required to register with the SEC under Advisers Act Section 203(b)(3). The U.S. Court of Appeals for the District of Columbia invalidated this rule in *Goldstein v. SEC*, No. 04-1434, 2006 (D.C. Cir. June 23, 2006).

Whether there is explicit deference to federal registration or the doctrine of federal supersession applies, advisers who are registered under the Advisers Act are entitled to take a performance allocation provided they comply with Advisers Act Rule 205-3, which generally allows an adviser to share in the profits of his or her client, provided the client meets certain qualifications. This test is part of the definition of "qualified client" under Rule 205-3. Under Advisers Act Rule 205-3, a qualified client is: a natural person or a company that, immediately after entering into the contract with the adviser has at least $750,000 under the management of the adviser (it doesn't have to be invested in one account; it can be spread among a number of different accounts managed by the same adviser); a natural person or company that the investment adviser reasonably believes, immediately prior to entering into the contract, either has a net worth (together with assets owned jointly with the investor's spouse) of more than $1.5 million, or a qualified purchaser as defined in § 2(a)(51)(A) of the Investment Company Act of 1940 (1940 Act) at the time the contract was entered into; or a natural person who, immediately prior to entering into the contract, is an executive officer, director, trustee, general partner, or person in a similar capacity of the investment adviser or is an employee of the investment adviser (other than someone performing clerical, secretarial, or administrative functions with regard to the investment adviser who, in connection with his or her regular functions or duties, participates in the investment activities of the adviser provided that such an employee has been

(continued...)

"Affiliate" or *"affiliate"* shall mean (i) any Person or entity, directly or indirectly controlling, controlled by or under common control with a specified Person or entity; (ii) any Person or entity owning or controlling ten percent (10%) or more of the outstanding voting securities of or interests in a specified entity; (iii) any employee, officer, director, partner or trustee of such specified Person or entity; and (iv) if a specified Person or entity is an officer, director, partner or trustee of a Person or entity, the Person or entity for which such Person or entity acts in such capacity.

"Affiliated Parties" shall have the meaning ascribed to it in 5.2(a).

"Agreement" shall mean this Limited Liability Company Agreement.

"Allocation Layer" or *"Layer"* shall mean, with respect to each Performance Year or Fiscal Period for each Member, each separate amount of Capital Contribution (i.e., layers) available for investment by the Company with respect to such Member on the applicable Investment Date, adjusted as necessary by the Member Manager to take into account withdrawals, Distributions, allocations of Net Profits and Net Losses, and such other items as the Member Manager deems necessary or appropriate in its sole discretion. The Member Manager shall allocate Net Profits (or Net Losses) to each Allocation Layer for purposes of computing the Performance Allocation. Notwithstanding the use of Allocation Layers for purposes of determining the Performance Allocation, each Member shall have only one Capital Account as required by Treasury Regulations. Further, at such time as one or more Allocation Layers no longer have significance in the

_____

(continued...)

performing such functions and duties for and on behalf of the investment adviser or substantially similar functions or duties for and on behalf of another company for at least twelve months.

While it is beyond the scope of this book to discuss the specific impact of registration under the Advisers Act, other than as described above, the person setting up hedge funds should carefully consider whether registration is required or perhaps advisable, as any "holding out" as an investment adviser could invite regulatory scrutiny and potential sanctions at both the state and federal level.

determination of a Performance Allocation, such Allocation Layers shall be combined by the Member Manager.[9]

"*Allocation Layer Percentage*" means, in respect of any Member for an Allocation Layer for a Fiscal Period, the percentage obtained by dividing the balance of such Member's Capital Account within such Allocation Layer by the total Capital Account of such Member.[10]

"*Applicable Federal Rate*" shall have the meaning ascribed to it in Section 7.10(c).

"*Arbitrator*" shall have the meaning ascribed to it in Section 13.6(a)(i).[11]

---

[9] Allocation layer or layers can masquerade under a variety of names. They can be called subaccounts, nominal accounts, series (but that must be distinguished from Series Funds, which are intended to provide ring-fenced insulation from liability on a series-to-series basis), or subclasses. The value of allocation layers, of course, is that they allow an investment manager to treat each contribution by an investor as a unique investment, and therefore allow the investment manager to take performance allocations with respect to each investment even though older investments may be "under water." This is a significant revision and improvement over the old omnibus "lost carry forward" accounts, which tend to account for losses collectively for each investor, preventing the manager from receiving a performance allocation with respect to a particular investor's account until all prior unrecovered losses for that investor have been recovered. Ultimately, it is a matter of negotiation between the investment manager/promoter of the Fund and the investors; an investment manager is wise to resist the temptation to provide omnibus loss carry forward protection. Allocation layers afford the manager the opportunity to "recreate" his or her Fund without having to redeem investors. As new money comes in, it is assigned to an allocation layer with a "high watermark" equal to the amount of investment, which is further adjusted as profits are realized.

[10] In an allocation layer structure, each layer has its own allocation layer percentage, which enables the administrator to allocate net profit to the Member's capital account within such allocation layer on a pro rata basis.

[11] The Model Agreement provides for an arbitrator to settle disputes. As set forth in § 13.6, this Section requires the use of arbitration proceedings in Wilmington, Delaware, along with a renunciation of any right to a trial by jury.

(continued...)

"Compensatory Interest" shall have the meaning ascribed to it in Section 7.7(a).[17]

"Designated Investment" shall have the meaning ascribed to it in Section 12.3(e).[18]

"Designated Investment Member" shall have the meaning ascribed to it in Section 12.3(f).

(continued...)

seizes the collateral, and then operates the collateral, and takes depreciation deductions that result in an increase in Minimum Gain, and then sells the property at a later point in time, these provisions may apply. It is hard to imagine, in the ordinary course, how financial assets could result in a tax basis that is less than an amount of nonrecourse liability secured by such financial assets without there first having been some realization event. Also, if a Fund had made a Section 754 and there is a transfer of an interest in the Fund at a loss, then Fund property tax basis will be reduced below the amount of debt giving rise to Minimum Gain. For this and other equally as compelling reasons, funds rarely make Section 754 elections. They also rarely allow transfers of interests, for this and a host of other securities and tax reasons. If the Fund invests in other funds, then there is an increased possibility of Minimum Gain being present.

[17] Compensatory Interest refers to any interest that is issued in exchange for services. While ordinarily a Fund is managed by a third-party manager under contract, there are ways in which a Compensatory Interest may be inadvertently issued, such as if placement agents are engaged in exchange for a share of partnership profits.

[18] The concept of "Designated Investments" is a new addition to the Model Agreement and is designed to deal with the creation of side pockets and similar liquidity management devices. A manager may choose to create a side pocket because it is hard to value assets held in the portfolio or because assets have either significantly increased or decreased in value as a result of market movements and the manager decides not to include that valuation as part of the asset mix for purposes of new investors coming into the portfolio. In order to maintain Designated Investment Accounts, the Fund's Operating Agreement must be able to support special allocations of profit and loss and all other tax attributes. The Designated Investment concept is designed to take those issues into account under a variety of circumstances.

"*Disposition*" shall have the meaning ascribed to it in Section 4.5(k)

"*Disputes*" shall have the meaning ascribed to it in Section 13.6(a).

"*Dispute Notice*" shall have the meaning ascribed to it in Section 13.6(a)(i).

"*Dissolution*" refers to the process by which the affairs of the Company are wound up resulting in the Termination of the Company. The Dissolution process is described in Article 11.[19]

"*Distribution*" shall mean any transfer of money or property to a Member, in its capacity as a Member, from the Company pursuant to this Agreement, including, but not limited to, any amount distributed to it upon its withdrawal from the Company or upon its withdrawal of a portion of its Capital Account.

"*ERISA*" shall mean the Employee Retirement Income Security Act of 1974, as amended from time to time.

"*Fair Value*" shall mean the fair value of all or a portion of the assets and/or investments of the Company as the context requires.

"*Feeder Fund(s)*" shall have the meaning ascribed to it in Section 5.5(e).

"*Final Reserve*" shall have the meaning ascribed to it in Section 4.5(e).

---

[19] While there have always been hedge Fund wind-ups, the rapid pace of Fund Dissolutions during the latter half of 2008 and the beginning of 2009 was truly astonishing. One of the key components of Dissolution procedures is making certain that the relative rights of all investors are preserved against predatory gun-jumping by certain investors who attempt to gain advantage by requesting withdrawal and then, perhaps, later withdrawing that request because the market has not turned as originally feared. The dire financial condition of 2008-2009 has forced creative reinterpretation of limited partnership agreements and LLC operating agreements in order to reach results consistent with the intended deal of the parties. A robust Dissolution-triggering mechanism coupled with the authority of the manager to take unilateral action when it makes sense to do so is essential.

"Final Withdrawal Amount" shall mean the remaining portion of the Withdrawal Amount, which shall be withdrawn on the Final Withdrawal Day.

"Final Withdrawal Day" shall mean the last day of the calendar quarter that commences immediately following the Initial Withdrawal Day.

"FINRA/NASD Rules" shall mean the Rules of FINRA (formerly, the National Association of Securities Dealers Inc.), as may be amended from time to time.

"Fiscal Period" shall mean the period of time beginning on the Closing Date and, thereafter, the day immediately following the end of a prior Fiscal Period and ending on the earliest of (i) the last day of each calendar month of the Fiscal Year, (ii) the day preceding the date any Member makes a Capital Contribution, (iii) the day on which any amount is debited to the Capital Account of any Member as a result of a Distribution (whether or not on account of a withdrawal of all or part of a Member's Capital Account pursuant to Section 4.1 or the compulsory withdrawal of all or part of a Member's Capital Account pursuant to Section 4.2) or (iv) the day on which the termination of the Company is completed pursuant to Article 11; but any period determined by reference to subsection (ii) or (iii) shall constitute a Fiscal Period only if treating such period as a Fiscal Period results in a Percentage Interest for any Member for such Fiscal Period which differs from such Member's Percentage Interest for the immediately preceding Fiscal Period. The initial Fiscal Period shall commence on the Closing Date.[20]

"Fiscal Year" shall mean the year ending June 30 or such date as the Member Manager may determine.

"Funds" shall have the meaning ascribed to it in Section 5.5(e).

---

[20] It is a constant source of amazement how something as simple as counting can trip up draftspersons, investors, and managers. The concept of the Fiscal Period and the need to treat as Fiscal Periods the stub period at the commencement of the life of the Fund and the stub period on the termination of an investment or of the Fund itself is necessary to the orderly operation of the Fund over time.

"GAAP" shall mean U.S. generally accepted accounting principles.[21]

"High Water Mark" shall have the meaning ascribed to it in Section 7.2(c)(i).

"Indemnified Parties" shall have the meaning ascribed to it in Section 5.8.

"Initial Reserve" shall have the meaning ascribed to it in Section 4.5(b).

"Initial Withdrawal Amount" shall mean 50 percent of the Withdrawal Amount, which shall be withdrawn on the Initial Withdrawal Day.

"Initial Withdrawal Day" shall have the meaning set forth in Section 4.1(b).

"Investment Company Act" shall mean the Investment Company Act of 1940, as amended from time to time.

"Investment Date" means the beginning of the Fiscal Year or of any Fiscal Period or the date of any additional Capital Contributions, in the case of existing Members, or the date of admission in the case of a new Member.[22]

---

[21] This Fund subscribes to U.S. generally accepted accounting principles. Showing once again the tangled web of the tax, securities, and accounting rules, the provision of GAAP financial statements has become virtually universal for advisers wishing to comply with the SEC's custody rules. An adviser registered under the Advisers Act is deemed to have "custody" if that adviser withdraws fees or otherwise has the authority to vest the assets of the Fund in any person. Clearly, an investment manager of any investment Fund would have that authority, and so technically such person is deemed to be a "custodian" under the federal securities laws. The primary consequence of that status is the need to conduct annual surprise audits and to provide statements to investors on a periodic basis. There is, however, a safe harbor for managers of hedge funds if they arrange to have audited GAAP financial statements delivered to their investors in a timely fashion (within 120 days following the close of the Fiscal Year of the Fund for single-strategy funds, and 180 days following the close of the Fiscal Year for funds of funds; *see* Advisers Act Rule 206(4)-2). If the financial statements are not audited in accordance with GAAP, then the manager must arrange for an annual surprise count. Failure to do so could potentially subject the adviser to penalties. These rules apply if an adviser is registered or required to be registered under Section 203 of the Advisers Act.

"Investment Manager" shall mean ABC Partners Inc., or such other entity as the Member Manager will determine from time to time in its sole discretion, to serve as the investment manager of the Company.

"JAMS" shall have the meaning ascribed to it in Section 13.6(a)(ii).[23]

"Liquidating Event" shall have the meaning ascribed thereto in Section 11.1.

"Liquidating Member" shall have the meaning ascribed thereto in Section 11.2.

"Majority in Interest of the Members" shall mean, at any time, Members who hold, in the aggregate, more than 50 percent (by value) of the Percentage Interests of all the Members, or such larger percentage as may be required by law for the specific purpose for which the Members are being polled.

"Management Fee" shall have the meaning ascribed to it in Section 5.4(a).

"Master Fund" shall mean ABC Master Fund Inc., an exempted company incorporated under the laws of the Cayman Islands.[24]

(continued...)

[22] Ordinarily, the Investment Date is deemed to commence immediately before the operation of business on that calendar day. The reason for that is so that the immediately preceding last business day's valuation can be used for purposes of determining the Percentage Interest of the Member when he makes an investment on a given day. Any other rule would require adoption of a full repricing strategy similar to that applicable to mutual funds, which allocate shares upon investment on the "next determined" closing price.

[23] This Model Agreement uses JAMS as the organization that provides arbitrators for resolving disputes under this Agreement. It could easily have been any of the other reputable arbitration societies or even a private arbitrator, as long as the parties agree.

[24] The ABC Fund, LLC is designed as a feeder Fund into the ABC Master Fund Inc., an exempt company incorporated under the laws of the Cayman Islands; but it also is designed to act as an operating Fund in its own right.

"Measurement Date" shall have the meaning ascribed to it in Section 12.1.

"Member" shall mean each Person executing this Agreement as a member of the Company and each Person who or which may hereafter become a party to this Agreement as provided herein.

"Membership Interest" shall mean the interest of a Member in the Company, which shall include the Member's Percentage Interest and Capital Account.

"Member Manager" shall mean ABC Partners Inc., or any other Person hereafter duly appointed or designated as the member manager pursuant to Section 5.16 to manage the business of the Company.[25]

"Net Asset Value" or *"NAV"* shall have the meaning ascribed to it in Section 12.1.

"Net Profits" and *"Net Losses"* means the amounts determined as follows:

> (a)   *"Net Profits"* for any Fiscal Period means (i) the sum of ((A) the Net Asset Value of the Company at the close of business on the last day of the Fiscal Period, increased by (B) any Distributions or withdrawals made with respect to such Fiscal Period), minus (ii) the sum of ((A) the Net Asset Value of the Company as of the close of business on the last day of the previous Fiscal Period, or in the case of the first Fiscal Period of the Fund, the Net Asset Value on the date the first contribution

---

[25] In this case, the Investment Manager is also the Member Manager of the Fund. While comparable to a general partner in a limited partnership, the roles of Member Manager and general partner do diverge. For example, a general partner has plenary authority to manage a limited partnership, including the appointment of investment advisers. A Member Manager may or may not have that authority, depending on the Operating Agreement, and the Member Manager may or may not be the Investment Manager, and the Member Manager may or may not have the authority to appoint or remove the Investment Manager. Another distinction is that a general partner is personally liable for the debts of the partnership; a Member Manager is not, absent some other reason for liability.

is made; plus (B) any additional Capital Contributions made during such Fiscal Period). Net Profits for any Performance Year shall be determined in the same manner as set forth in the previous sentence except that the term "Performance Year" shall be substituted for "Fiscal Period" wherever that term appears.

(b)   *"Net Losses"* for any Fiscal Period means (i) the sum of ((A) the Net Asset Value of the Company at the close of business on the last day of the previous Fiscal Period or in the case of the first Fiscal Period of the Fund, the Net Asset Value on the date the first contribution is made; plus (B) any additional Capital Contributions made during such Fiscal Period), minus (ii) the sum of ((A) the Net Asset Value of the Company as of the close of business on the last day of such Fiscal Period, increased by (B) any Distributions or withdrawals made with respect to such Fiscal Period). Net Losses for any Performance Year shall be determined in the same manner as set forth in the previous sentence except that the term "Performance Year" shall be substituted for "Fiscal Period" wherever that term appears.

The definitions of Net Profits and Net Losses are intended to comply with the provisions of Treas. Reg. §1.704-1(b)(2)(iv) (including, without limitation, Treas. Reg. §§ 1.704-1(b)(2)(iv)*(d)*, 1.704-1(b)(2)(iv)*(f)* and 1.704-1(b)(2)(iv)*(g)*) and shall be interpreted consistently therewith. It is intended that the Net Profits or Net Losses allocated for each Fiscal Period will consist of the aggregate of all items of income, gain, loss, deduction and expense of the Company (other than the Management Fee) required to be allocated to the Capital Accounts of the Members pursuant to the provisions of Treas. Reg. 1.704-1(b)(2)(iv), including unrealized gain and loss on the assets and/or investments of the Company pursuant to revaluations at the end of each Fiscal Period under Treas. Reg. 1.704-1(b)(2)(iv)*(f)*. In the event that the amount of Net Profits or Net Losses differs from the amount of items required to be allocated to the Capital Accounts of the Members under the provisions of Treas. Reg. 1.704-1(b)(2)(iv), the Manager shall make such adjustments to the allocations of items as the Manager deems appropriate in accordance with Section 7.1(a) hereof.

"Nonrecourse Deductions" has the meaning set forth in §1.704-2(b)(1) of the Treasury Regulations.

"Nonrecourse Liability" has the meaning set forth in §1.704-2(b)(3) of the Treasury Regulations.

"Offering Memorandum" shall mean the Company's Confidential Private Placement Memorandum dated July 2009, as amended, modified, and supplemented from time to time.[26]

"Organizational Expenses" shall mean any fees, costs, and expenses of or incidental to the formation and organization of the Company, including

---

[26] The ultimate contractual status of a private placement memorandum has been debated among professionals for a long time. Is it merely a disclosure document; or does it form some form of quasi-contract because of the reliance placed upon it by investors? In other words, can a private placement memorandum modify an operating agreement? The answer should be and is yes. If investors invest in reliance on a statement made in the private placement memorandum, and if that private placement memorandum was issued at or about the same time as the operating agreement, it is doubtful a litigant would have to prove ambiguity or uncertainty on the face of the operating agreement for a court to impute the provisions of the offering memorandum into the agreement between the parties. As an offering memorandum evolves, there is always the question of whether subsequent modifications can nevertheless act to modify contrary terms of the operating agreement. If a situation arises with that drafting disconnect, the best recourse is to conform the documents and if need be modify the operating agreement so that it is consistent with the expectations of the parties. If that is unpalatable to the manager or the management team, the manager will be required to elicit the consent of the investors if the matter is a material item. For this reason, the amendment provisions of this operating agreement allow for unilateral amendment, and where the impact of such an amendment would have a material adverse effect, it requires a majority vote. *See infra.*

fees, costs, and expenses incurred for administrative, legal, accounting, filing, printing, and travel and entertainment purposes.[27]

"*Partner Nonrecourse Debt*" has the meaning set forth in §1.704-2(b)(4) of the Treasury Regulations.

"*Partner Nonrecourse Debt Minimum Gain*" means an amount, with respect to each Partner Nonrecourse Debt, equal to the Company Minimum Gain that would result if such Partner Nonrecourse Debt were treated as a Nonrecourse Liability, determined in accordance with §1.704-2(i)(3) of the Treasury Regulations.

"*Partner Nonrecourse Deductions*" has the meaning set forth in §§1.704-2(i)(1) and 1.704-2(i)(2) of the Treasury Regulations.

"*Partnership Minimum Gain*" has the meaning set forth in §§1.704-2(b)(2) and 1.704-2(d) of the Treasury Regulations.

"*Percentage Interest*" with respect to any Member for any Fiscal Period, shall mean the amount, expressed as a percentage, determined by dividing the aggregate balance of such Member's Capital Account on the relevant day of such Fiscal Period (ordinarily the last day of such period) by the sum of the

---

[27] This omnibus definition of Organizational Expenses must be further broken down among pre-opening expenses, document organizational costs, and syndication costs for tax purposes. Once again, there is a divergence between tax and accounting rules. U.S. GAAP ordinarily requires the immediate expensing of organizational costs and pre-opening costs. This is to prevent prepaid expenses on the balance sheet, inflating that asset value, when, in fact, there is little value attributable to such expenditures once a Fund is closed. Allowing such assets to remain on the books of the firm could potentially inflate the net asset value of the firm. The Code, on the other hand, requires these expenditures to be amortized pro rata over 180 months (fifteen years), resulting in a book tax differential. This is ameliorated somewhat to the extent that the Code allows immediate expensing of up to $5,000 of startup costs and $5,000 of organizational costs. The remaining amounts need to be amortized. Another key factor to consider is the requirement that syndication costs be separately accounted for. Such costs are neither deductible nor amortizable. Generally, these relate to the preparation of the offering memorandum itself and various private placement activities.

aggregate balances of the Capital Accounts of all the Members on such day, and multiplying the result by 100 (i.e., expressed as a percentage).[28]

"Performance Allocation" shall have the meaning ascribed to it in Section 7.2(c).

"Performance Year" shall mean (a) the calendar year; or (b) the period commencing on the first day of operations and thereafter on the first day of the calendar year and ending on the occurrence of a Liquidating Event; or (c) the period commencing on the day after the occurrence of a Liquidating Event and ending on the earlier to occur of the end of the calendar year and the date of Termination, or (d) the period commencing on the first day of a calendar year and ending on the date of Termination.

"Person" shall mean any natural person, corporation, company, governmental authority, limited liability company, partnership, trust, estate, association, unincorporated association, custodian, nominee, or other entity or organization in its own or in any representative capacity.

"Plan Assets" shall have the meaning ascribed to it in Section 13.9(b).

"Preliminary Amount" shall have the meaning ascribed to it in Section 7.2(a).

"Proposed Rules" shall have the meaning ascribed to it in Section 7.7(a).

"Required Interest" of the Members means 66 percent or greater Percentage Interest of the Members.

"Revocation Fee" shall have the meaning ascribed to it in Section 4.1(c)

"Safe Harbor Election" shall have the meaning ascribed to it in Section 7.7(a).

"Schedule of Members" shall have the meaning ascribed to it in the recitals.

---

[28] Percentage Interest is a mechanical but dynamic computation based on the relevant period for which it is being computed.

"Securities" (or singularly, *Security*) shall mean common stock (and securities convertible into common stock), preferred stock (and securities convertible into preferred stock), general or limited partnership interests or other shares of, or participations in, equity or beneficial interests, debentures, notes or bonds (which may or may not be convertible into equity securities), commercial paper, bills, other evidences of indebtedness (including whole loans), commodities, commodities contracts, commodity futures, financial futures, futures contracts, certificates, receipts, certificates of interest in any profit-sharing agreement, collateral trust certificates, reorganization certificates, subscriptions, investment contracts, voting trust certificates, certificates of deposit, other short-term fixed-income securities, money market funds, swap contracts, bankers acceptances, repurchase agreements, currencies, forward contracts for such currencies, options relating to a securities index, and indexes relating to any of the foregoing, or interim certificates for, receipts for, guarantees of, or warrants, put or call options or rights to subscribe to or purchase, any of the foregoing or currencies, or any other instruments or interests in the nature of securities or investments of any kind whatsoever, whether issued in public offerings or private placements, of any type issued or created by any Person, corporation, partnership, trust, firm, public authority (including, without limitation, the United States, any state thereof or any foreign country, or by any agency, subdivision, territory, dependency, possession or municipality, including any agency of a municipality), or organization of any kind organized under the laws of the United States or of any state, territory, dependency or possession thereof or of any foreign country, or of any subdivision, territory, dependency, possession or municipality thereof, or supranational organization, without regard to the business carried on by such corporation or business organization or to the part of the world where it is carried on or where such corporation or business organization is organized.[29]

"Shareholder" refers to a person who is a Member of the Company pursuant to Article 3.

"Side Pocket Account" shall have the meaning ascribed to it in Section 12.3.

---

[29] The definition of Security is parroted from the Investment Company Act of 1940 definition.

"*Special Assets*" shall mean assets and/or investments that are illiquid, hard to value, and/or nonperforming.

"*Start-up Expenses*" shall mean any fees, costs, and expenses of the Company incurred in connection with the investigation, analysis and acquisition of initial investments and trades by the Company in anticipation of the Company engaging in an active trade or business.[30]

"*Syndication Expenses*" shall mean expenses that are classified as "Syndication Expenses" pursuant to Treas. Reg. § 1.709-2(b).[31]

"*Tax Matters Partner*" shall have the meaning ascribed to it in Section 8.2.

"*Tentative Distributions*" shall have the meaning ascribed to it in Section 7.10(a)

"*Termination*" shall have the meaning ascribed to it in Section 11.8.

"*Transfer*" shall have the meaning ascribed to it in Section 9.1.

"*Treasury Regulations*" or "*Treas. Reg.*" shall mean all proposed, temporary or final treasury regulations promulgated under the Code as from time to time in effect.

"*Unrecovered Losses*" shall have the meaning ascribed to it in Section 7.2(c)(viii).[32]

"*Void Transfer*" shall have the meaning ascribed to it in Section 9.1(e).

---

[30] This definition of Start-up Expenses dovetails with the definition of Organizational Expenses discussed at footnote 27.

[31] Syndication Expenses, of course, refer to those expenses incurred in the promotion and sale of the Securities issued by the Fund. These are subjected to a special tax status under the Internal Revenue Code and the appropriate regulations of Subchapter K thereof.

[32] The Unrecovered Losses are assigned to specific Allocation Layers under the Model Agreement.

"*Withdrawal Amount*" means the amount requested to be withdrawn by a Member pursuant to a Withdrawal Request pursuant to Section 4.1 or 4.2, as the case may be.

"*Withdrawal Date*" shall have the meaning ascribed to it in Section 4.1(b).

"*Withdrawal Day*" shall mean, with respect to any Withdrawing Member, the Initial Withdrawal Day, and/or the Final Withdrawal Day.

"*Withdrawal Request*" shall have the meaning ascribed to it in Section 4.1(b).

"*Withdrawing Member*" means a Member who is withdrawing all or any part of his Capital Account.

ARTICLE 2
ORGANIZATION

2.1   Formation. The Company was formed as a Delaware limited liability company by the filing of the Company's Certificate of Formation in the Office of the Secretary of State of Delaware in accordance with the Act. Gregory J. Nowak, Esq. and Pepper Hamilton LLP are authorized to act as formation agent to prepare, sign, and file all documents incident to the formation of the Company, and to be indemnified by the Company with respect to such service rendered.

2.2   Name. The name of the Company shall be "ABC Fund, LLC" or such other name as the Member Manager may determine in accordance with the Act. The Company may cause appropriate trade name and similar statements to be filed and published under the name set forth in this Section 2.2, or such other names as the Company may have or use in any jurisdiction from time to time.[33]

---

[33] As a matter of best practices, I always make it a point to do an Internet search using a robust browser to determine if the name chosen has been used by some competing enterprise. In a rare case, you may be surprised to see what you find. In a recent matter, after having conducted an Internet search on a proposed name, we determined that the name had actually represented a prior investment firm that had

(continued...)

2.3   Principal Place of Business and Registered Office and Agent. The principal place of business of the Company shall be ABC Partners Inc., _____, or such other place as the Member Manager may in its sole discretion designate from time to time.

The address of the registered office of the Company in the State of Delaware shall be c/o PHS Corporate Services Inc., 1313 Market Street, Suite 5100, Wilmington, Delaware 19899-1709. The name and address of the registered agent for service of process on the Company in the State of Delaware shall be c/o PHS Corporate Services Inc., 1313 Market Street, Suite 5100, Wilmington, Delaware 19899-1709, or such other registered office, agent, or address as the Member Manager may in its sole discretion designate from time to time.[34]

2.4   Qualification in Other Jurisdictions. The Member Manager shall cause the Company to be qualified to do business or registered under assumed or fictitious name statutes or similar laws in any jurisdiction in which such qualification or registration is required or desirable, and shall

_____

(continued...)

been accused of managing a Ponzi scheme. The founder of that former firm had also been found murdered.

Further, it might make sense to attempt to protect the intellectual property of the firm by trademarking the name, or at least its uncommon root, in order to provide a basis for defending the name and the franchise at a later date. Please consult experienced intellectual property counsel.

[34] The ABC Fund LLC uses the corporate office services of an affiliate of Pepper Hamilton LLP. The registered agent acts to accept service of process for the Company in the state of Delaware. When engaging the registered agent, it is imperative that arrangements be made for the timely forwarding of franchise tax bills and all other correspondence. Failure to do so can cause significant headaches later, such as, for example, when a Fund needs to obtain a good standing certificate (such as in order to participate in a government program such as the TALF lending programs initiated by the Federal Reserve Bank of New York in the fall of 2008 to help combat the financial crisis of 2008-2009).

execute, deliver and file any certificates (and any amendments and/or restatements thereof) necessary to effect such qualification or registration.[35]

2.5   _Term_. The term of the Company commenced upon the date of filing of the Certificate of Formation pursuant to the Act, and shall continue in full force and effect until Termination pursuant to Section 11.8 hereof.

2.6   _Purpose_. The Company's business and general purpose is to engage in any lawful act or activity for which a limited liability company may be organized under the Act, including without limitation, to trade, buy, sell, spread, swap, acquire, hold, or dispose of:

> (a)   capital stock, shares of beneficial interest, distressed and technically stressed fixed income securities, whole loan mortgages, asset-backed securities, real estate bridge loans, structured notes, collateralized mortgage obligations, mortgage-backed securities, and derivative instruments relating thereto, warrants, bonds, notes, debentures, whether subordinated, convertible or otherwise, directly managed accounts, open-end and closed-end mutual funds, partnership interests, money market funds, commercial paper, certificates of deposit, bank debt, trade claims, obligations of the United States or any State thereof or any other government, bankers' acceptances, trust receipts and other obligations, and instruments or evidences of indebtedness commonly referred to as securities of whatever kind or nature of any person,

---

[35] Often overlooked is the need for a Fund to qualify to do business wherever it actually does business. Of course, traditionally investment funds were not deemed to engage in a trade or business. The local laws of every jurisdiction in which an adviser representative of the Fund resides or has a principal place of business should be checked along, of course, with the principal offices of the Manager and Investment Manager.

corporation, partnership, trust, limited liability company, government or entity whatsoever;

(b)   rights and options relating thereto, whether readily marketable or not;

(c)   commodity futures contracts, forward contracts, options, "spot" transactions and swap arrangements involving stock indexes or other indexes, financial instruments, interest rates, currencies or any other contract or property which may be the subject of a swap arrangement, equity credit or currency derivative and any combination of these investments, transactions, or instruments; and

(d)   any other Securities, investments or instruments.

The Company may engage in the foregoing activities either directly or through other investment vehicles, subsidiaries, or affiliates, including but not limited to making direct investments in wholly owned subsidiaries that may engage in financing or similar businesses.[36]

---

[36] Consistent with the "kitchen sink" approach of the Model Agreement, the purpose clause in Section 2.6 is drafted extremely broadly and allows investment in "everything." The last paragraph authorizes the Company not only to engage in direct investment, but also to use other investment vehicles, including subsidiaries. This is significant if, for example, the Fund decides to participate in the TALF program of the New York Federal Reserve Bank or similar program by creating a special purpose subsidiary that would be the TALF borrower, or, for example, if the Fund chooses to invest in certain structured securities where the character of the income being thrown off by such security may or may not be consistent with the character sought by the investors in the Fund. A wholly owned subsidiary that would hold such investments is a useful means of mitigating the impact of such investments.

ARTICLE 3
MEMBERS

3.1   Names and Address. The names and addresses of the Members shall be set forth in the books and records of the Company.

3.2   Limitation of Liability. Except as required by law, and as otherwise provided in this Agreement, the debts, obligations and liabilities of the Company, whether arising in contract, tort or otherwise, shall be solely the debts, obligations and liabilities of the Company, and no Member or Member Manager shall be obligated personally for any such debt, obligation or liability of the Company solely by reason of being a Member or acting as a Member Manager of the Company. Nothing in this Agreement shall constitute a waiver by any party of any non-waivable right that an investor enjoys under federal or state law.[37]

3.3   Membership Interests.

> (a)   Except as otherwise required by law, Membership Interests shall be fully paid and nonassessable upon receipt by the Company of the agreed Capital Contributions with respect thereto.

> (b)   Except as required by law, and as otherwise provided in this Agreement with respect to amendments hereof and the Dissolution of the Company, no Membership Interest will be deemed to confer any voting rights on a Member with respect to the Company, except with regard to the Member Manager who shall hold all voting shares. No Member shall have priority over any other Member except as herein provided. This Section 3.3(b) shall

---

[37] Section 3.3 is in homage to our federal system of government. While for state law purposes a Member may not be obligated personally for any debt of the Company and may not have any liability to any other Member of the Company, it is necessary to include the last sentence of Section 3.2 to make it clear that federal securities laws could, in the appropriate case, trump such limitation of liability.

not apply to repayment of any loan or other indebtedness made by a Member to the Company.

(c)   In certain instances herein, Members are referred to as "Partners" and the Company is referred to as the "Partnership." This is done for the sake of clarity as the federal and state income tax status of the Company as a partnership necessarily requires the application of the partnership tax rules to this Agreement and the operations of the Company.

ARTICLE 4
WITHDRAWALS[38]

4.1   <u>Withdrawal by Members.</u>

(a)   No Member shall be entitled to withdraw any amount from its Capital Account or withdraw from the Company, except as otherwise provided in this Article 4. To the extent a Member is permitted to withdraw all or a portion of its Capital Account or to withdraw from the Company, the interest of such Member shall continue to be subject to the same risks as other Members until the date of actual withdrawal or earlier termination of the Company except as specified herein.[39]

---

[38] No provisions of an operating agreement come under scrutiny like the withdrawal provisions in a time of economic turbulence. If managers have only limited time and resources to focus on their operating agreement, it is imperative that they spend a significant portion of it on the withdrawal section.

[39] The last sentence of Section 4.1(a) is designed to make clear that until a Member's interest or part thereof withdrawn is fully extinguished, the Member remains subject to the risks of the Fund until the actual withdrawal or earlier termination of the Fund. Merely because an investor has put in a withdrawal notice,

(continued...)

(b)   Subject to Section 4.10 hereof and the overall 20 percent withdrawal limitation each discussed below, a Member may, in accordance with and subject to the applicable provisions of this Agreement and applicable law, withdraw all or a portion of its Capital Account as of the last Business Day of a calendar quarter or such other days as may be determined by the Member Manager (a *Withdrawal Date*), pursuant to written notice (a *Withdrawal* Request), stating the amount to be withdrawn, which must be received by the Company at least ninety (90) days prior to such Withdrawal Date (the *Initial Withdrawal Day*) with respect to the Initial Withdrawal Amount less the Initial Reserve. [40]

(c)   Effective upon the Initial Withdrawal Day, the Withdrawing Member shall become a creditor of the Company with respect to the Initial Withdrawal Amount, <u>less</u> the Initial Reserve. Effective upon the Final Withdrawal Day, the Withdrawing Member shall become a creditor of the Company with respect to the Final Withdrawal

---

(continued...)

and may even have received some proceeds, does not change the fact that to the extent that any proceeds remain in the Fund, the investment remains at risk. The Member does not enjoy a creditor's status, unless otherwise specified in the Agreement.

[40] This is a fairly standard withdrawal provision: quarterly liquidity as of the last business day of the calendar quarter with at least ninety days' prior notice. Managers should be wary of waiving the time deadlines of these provisions. If someone is late getting a notice of withdrawal to the manager, the appropriate response is to push that withdrawal to the next quarterly withdrawal date because the ninety-day notice was not met. The defined terms used in this section are very important to determining the relative rights and responsibilities of the parties. Note that the Initial Withdrawal Day is at least ninety days prior to the withdrawal date.

Amount, <u>less</u> the Final Reserve.[41] In the event that the Member Manager allows a Member to revoke its Withdrawal Request, the Withdrawing Member shall pay to the Company a revocation fee in an amount equal to 2 percent of the amount that would have been withdrawn if the Withdrawal Request had not been revoked (the "*Revocation Fee*"). See examples at Section 4.5(m).[42]

(d)   In the event a Member withdraws any of its Capital Account prior to the one-year anniversary of the date of any particular Capital Contribution, such Member will pay the Company a withdrawal fee of 15.0 percent of the Withdrawal Amount computed after the application of the Performance Allocation and after payment of all expenses including any

---

[41] The Withdrawing Member becomes a creditor with respect to the Initial Withdrawal Amount on the Initial Withdrawal Day <u>less</u> the Initial Reserve. Similarly, the Withdrawing Member becomes a creditor of the Company with respect to the Final Withdrawal Amount less the Final Reserve on the Final Withdrawal Date.

[42] To eliminate the gamesmanship present with someone using the withdrawal mechanism to gain advantage, the ABC Fund Agreement imposes a 2 percent charge on the Withdrawing Member in the form of a revocation fee of the amount that would have been withdrawn if the withdrawal request had not been revoked. Such fees, of course, inure to the benefit of the Fund and therefore are used to compensate the other investors because assets had been liquidated in order to meet the Withdrawal Request. These types of provisions, however, need to walk a very thin tightrope, because any burden on the right to terminate an advisory contract (such as a termination fee) is generally given a dim view by the Securities and Exchange Commission. As this is a sale of a security, there is a different analysis. Contingent deferred sales charges have traditionally been acceptable in the mutual Fund context, for example, but an early termination fee on an advisory contract with a separate account generally is not acceptable. *See, e.g., National Deferred Compensation (pub. avail. Aug. 31, 1987)* ("an adviser may not fulfill its fiduciary obligations if it imposes a fee structure penalizing a client for deciding to terminate the adviser's service or if it imposes an additional fee on a client for choosing to change his investment").

Management Fees.[43] In addition, if a Member withdraws any of its Capital Account on or after the one year anniversary of the date of any particular Capital Contribution and prior to the two year anniversary of the date of such Capital Contribution, such Member will pay the Company a withdrawal fee of 5.0 percent of the Withdrawal Amount computed after the application of the Performance Allocation and after payment of all expenses including any Management Fees. All Withdrawal Requests received with respect to a particular Withdrawal Date shall be treated *pari passu* regardless of the date the Withdrawal Request is received by the Company.[44]

(e)   In addition to its authority to suspend withdrawals (as discussed in further detail below), the Member Manager of the Company, following consultation with the Investment Manager, may, in its sole and absolute discretion, defer withdrawals for any Withdrawal Date where Withdrawal Requests in the aggregate exceed 20 percent of the value of

---

[43] Section 4.1(d) also imposes a contingent-deferred sales charge in the amount of 15 percent of the Withdrawal Amount in the event that the withdrawal occurs prior to the one-year anniversary of the date of the particular capital contribution. For purposes of clarity, the Agreement specifies that the Withdrawal Fee is paid to the Company (*i.e.*, the Fund), and it is computed after the application of the performance allocation and after the payment of all expenses, including any management fees attributable to the interest withdrawn. This Withdrawal Fee is reduced to 5 percent of the amount withdrawn for any withdrawal that occurs after the one-year anniversary and prior to the two-year anniversary. These types of economic burdens are in lieu of lockups, generally, under the theory that investors who truly want their money back will be willing to pay a financial penalty to do so rather than allow their money to remain at risk.

[44] All Withdrawal Requests must be treated the same along with all other Withdrawal Requests that are made with respect to a particular Withdrawal Date. Favoring one investor over another under these circumstances is to be avoided.

the Company's net assets and/or investments on such Withdrawal Date.[45] In these circumstances, the Member Manager, following consultation with the Investment Manager, may scale down *pro rata* the amount requested to be withdrawn in response to each Withdrawal Request to such extent as is necessary to ensure that the foregoing limit is not exceeded and shall carry forward the balance for withdrawal to the next Withdrawal Date, and so on to each next succeeding Withdrawal Date until each Withdrawal Request has been complied with in full. Withdrawal Requests that have been carried forward from an earlier period (and not withdrawn) shall have priority over later Withdrawal Requests.[46] If a Member's Withdrawal Request has been scaled down in accordance with this Section 4.1(e), such Member shall remain a Member of the Company, and such Member's Capital Account, including any deferred Withdrawal Amount under this Section 4.1(e), shall be allocated Net Profits and Net Losses and charged Management Fees and Performance Allocations, until such time as such

---

[45] Section 4.1(e) evidences one of the "post-2008 Fund" provisions. The maximum amount that can be withdrawn is 20 percent of the value of the Company's net assets or investments on the Withdrawal Date. The Member Manager, in consultation with the Investment Manager, has the discretion to impose this 20 percent limit. This authority is in addition to the Member Manager's authority to suspend withdrawals unilaterally as it sees fit.

[46] Any Withdrawal Request that is scaled down to meet the limitations is carried forward to the next Withdrawal Date. This Agreement uses a priority system that requires redemption notices received first in time to have priority over later notices until, serially, all Withdrawal Requests are satisfied. Under this provision, if a Withdrawal Request has been scaled down, then the amount shall continue to be at risk in the Fund, shall be allocated net profits and losses, and charged management fees and performance allocations until such time as the Member is permitted to actually withdraw the Member's entire capital account.

Member has been permitted to withdraw such Member's entire Capital Account.

(f)   Due to the separate calculation of the Performance Allocation as to each Allocation Layer, it is possible that, if a Member owns multiple Allocation Layers, a withdrawal of one Allocation Layer will result in the payment of a Performance Allocation to the Member Manager, while withdrawal of a different Allocation Layer would not, but would result in the reduction of the losses that must be recovered before the Member Manager may receive a Performance Allocation as to that Allocation Layer.[47]

(g)   With respect to any Withdrawal Date, a Member can withdraw either: (a) part, rather than all, of such Member's Capital Account, but only if such Member's remaining Capital Account is at least $1 million; or (b) all of such Member's Capital Account. The minimum withdrawal amount is $250,000 or all of a Member's Capital Account; minimums are subject to decrease or waiver in the sole discretion of the Member Manager.[48]

(h)   Unless a Member specifies otherwise in the Member's written Withdrawal Request, upon a

---

[47] This section evidences the true elegance of the Allocation Layer accounting method. As Members can specifically identify which performance Allocation Layer they wish to redeem, they can choose either to allow low High Water Mark assets to remain in the Fund and pay Performance Allocations or redeem such assets in an attempt first to recoup unrecovered losses with respect to a particular Allocation Layer.

[48] Minimum ongoing deposits in a Fund are becoming much more commonplace as managers wrestle with the fact that the market downturn has, in many instances, imperiled the viability of funds with low amounts of assets. Requiring a minimal capital balance and minimum Withdrawal Amounts is not uncommon.

partial withdrawal by a Member, the withdrawal will be allocated among the Allocation Layers on a first-in first-out basis.[49] Following a partial withdrawal of a Member's Capital Account, the High Water Mark and Unrecovered Losses with respect to the Allocation Layers thereof not withdrawn shall be reduced *pro tanto* by an amount equal to that Member's High Water Mark or Unrecovered Losses, as the case may be, with respect to the Allocation Layers from which the withdrawal was made multiplied by the amount withdrawn divided by the Member's total Capital Account prior to the withdrawal.

(i) None of the withdrawal from the Company, death, disability, incompetency, termination, bankruptcy, insolvency, or dissolution of a Member, shall dissolve the Company. The legal representatives of a Member shall succeed as assignee to the Member's interest in the Company upon the death, disability, incompetency, termination, bankruptcy, insolvency or dissolution of a Member, but shall not be admitted as a substitute Member without the prior written consent of the Member Manager.

(j) The Member Manager may, in its sole discretion, modify or waive any of the withdrawal requirements or limitations set forth in this Section 4.1, including, but not limited to the withdrawal fee, either for Members generally or for particular Members, and either at the time a

---

[49] Section 4.1(h) allows a Member to apply specific identification to manage both tax consequences and High Water Marks. If no designation is made, a first-in first-out (FIFO) method is used.

particular withdrawal is proposed or in advance by agreement with one or more Members.[50]

4.2   <u>Compulsory Withdrawal</u>.[51] The Member Manager may, with or without cause, in its sole discretion, require any Member to withdraw its entire Capital Account or a portion thereof from the Company, at any time for any reason or for no reason on not less than five (5) calendar days' notice, such termination to be effective on the date specified in such notice. Payment shall be made in accordance with the procedure applicable to voluntary withdrawals where the date specified in the notice is treated as an Initial Withdrawal Day.

4.3   <u>Consequences upon Withdrawal</u>.

(a)   Upon any Member's withdrawal of the entire balance of his or its Capital Account pursuant to Section 4.1 or 4.2:

(i)   such Withdrawing Member shall withdraw from the Company as of the Final Withdrawal Day;

(ii)   the Member Manager shall amend the Schedule of Members to reflect the withdrawal of such Withdrawing Member; and

---

[50] The Member Manager is entitled to waive the provisions governing withdrawals in an appropriate case.

[51] Hedge Fund managers, especially managers of so-called 3(c)(1) funds, need the ability to protect the Investment Company Act status of their fund. The Compulsory Withdrawal provisions are designed to allow the Manager to do just that, but also to protect the Fund in the event of an "anti-money laundering" violation, to enable the Manager to create "head room" under investor caps, to eliminate unaccredited investors, and to eliminate nonqualified purchasers in so-called 3(c)(7) funds. These provisions are also used to terminate the Fund as necessary, especially when the agreement has been drafted to require the consent of investors to material changes.

(iii)   such Withdrawing Member's Percentage
          Interest shall be zero on and after the first
          day of the first Fiscal Period commencing
          after such Member's Final Withdrawal Day,
          and such Withdrawing Member's Capital
          Account balance shall be deemed to be zero
          as of such first day for the purpose of
          determining the Percentage Interests of the
          Members   for   any   Fiscal   Period
          commencing after the Final Withdrawal
          Day.[52]

(b)   Upon any Member's withdrawal of less than the
        entire balance of the Member's Capital Account
        pursuant to Section 4.1 or 4.2, such Member's
        Percentage Interest shall be reduced to reflect
        such Member's continuing interest in the
        Company, and such Member's Capital Account
        balance shall likewise be adjusted. All such
        adjustments shall be done in such a manner and at
        such time so that on and after the first day of the
        first Fiscal Period commencing after such
        Member's partial withdrawal, the Percentage
        Interests and Allocation Layers of the Members
        properly reflect such partial withdrawal, in
        accordance with Section 4.1(h).[53]

---

[52] While the consequences set forth in Section 4.3(a) may appear to restate the
obvious, it is not inconceivable for an investor to attempt to argue for some
residual value, especially if a Fund experiences a significant windfall after the Final
Withdrawal Day of an investor. This provision forecloses that residual argument.

[53] This provision allows a proper realignment of the Fund's capital accounts and
Percentage Interests. Such adjustments, of course, must be done in good faith with
a view to fairness to all.

4.4   Adjustment of Capital Accounts.

        (a)   Even if the Withdrawal Day of a Member is not the last day of any Performance Year, the Member Manager shall be entitled to a Performance Allocation with respect to each Allocation Layer being withdrawn by such Member (or, in the case of a partial withdrawal, that portion of the Allocation Layer withdrawn as determined by the Member Manager), calculated as though the applicable Withdrawal Day was the last day of the Performance Year;[54] provided, however, that in the case of a partial withdrawal, the Member Manager may, in its sole discretion, elect to delay taking the Performance Allocation until the end of the Performance Year;[55] and further provided that the Net Profit upon which such Performance Allocation is determined pursuant to this Section 4.4(a) shall not include any Net Profits upon which a Performance Allocation is determined pursuant to Section 7.2(c). In the case of a partial withdrawal by or of a Member, the Member Manager shall reasonably determine the amount of Net Profits (if any) and the Performance Allocation attributable to that portion of such Allocation Layer to which such partial withdrawal relates.

---

[54] This provision is intended to protect the Manager from an unscrupulous investor who would attempt to withdraw before a computation date for a Performance Allocation. Whenever an investor withdraws, it is as if the Fund's Fiscal Year had closed on the date of withdrawal, and profit and loss for that period is computed.

[55] The Model Agreement provides a unique provision allowing the Manager to delay taking the Performance Allocation with respect to the partial withdrawal of an Allocation Layer until the end of the Performance Year. Note that the amount of the Performance Allocation is fixed on the date of withdrawal. Only the payment allocation to the Manager is deferred.

(b)   All expenses described in Section 4.7 in connection with the withdrawal shall be charged to the Capital Account of the Withdrawing Member.[56]

(c)   If, after the Capital Accounts of the Members have been adjusted pursuant to Section 4.4(a) with respect to any Withdrawal Day, the Withdrawing Member's Capital Account has a negative balance, the Withdrawing Member shall receive no Distribution pursuant to Section 4.5 and an amount equal to such negative balance shall be credited to such Withdrawing Member's Capital Account and shall be allocated to the Capital Accounts of the Members (other than the Withdrawing Member) in accordance with Section 7.2 as if such amount constituted Net Losses or other Company expenses for the Fiscal Period beginning after the Withdrawal Day, and, for the avoidance of doubt, in no event shall any Member be required to or liable to restore any such negative Capital Account balance to the Company on the liquidation of the Company.[57]

---

[56] The costs of withdrawal, including legal opinions, brokerage, and other issues, are all charged to the Withdrawing Member. This is designed to protect the ongoing investors in the Fund from the expenses associated with accommodating investor withdrawals. Of course, such expense allocations are viewed as special allocations under the tax rules, which require that the partnership agreement allocations have substantial economic effect.

[57] Section 4.4(c) reinforces that, for the avoidance of doubt, no Member can be required to restore a negative capital account balance, regardless of how that negative balance is created. Members of the limited liability company have at risk only their capital accounts (the sum of their investments, and allocated gains less withdrawals less allocated losses, whether or not such gains and losses are realized because of the book-up/book down provisions).

4.5   <u>Distribution upon Withdrawal</u>.[58]

(a)   (i)   Upon a withdrawal of a Member's entire Membership Interest, such Member shall generally receive payments calculated based on the value of its Capital Account as of the end of the Fiscal Period that ends on the Initial Withdrawal Day as to 50 percent of the Membership Interest to be withdrawn on the Initial Withdrawal Day, subject to the provisions of this Article 4 and Article 7. In addition, such Member shall generally receive payments calculated based on the value of its Capital Account as of the end of the Fiscal Period that ends on the Final Withdrawal Day as to the remaining portion of the Membership Interest to be withdrawn on the Final Withdrawal Day. The actual amount paid and the timing of payment is subject to the holdback for reserves described below.

(ii)   Upon a Member's withdrawal of a portion of its Membership Interest, such Member shall receive a proportionate share of the amount it would have received if the Member had withdrawn its entire Membership Interest, allocated among Capital Contributions, undistributed profit and all other amounts included in the Capital Account of the Member on a pro rata basis.

---

[58] The payment procedures outlined in the Model Agreement in the event of a withdrawal are designed to minimize the cash impact on the Fund. *See* examples below.

(b)   On the last Business Day of the next calendar quarter following the Initial Withdrawal Day pursuant to Sections 4.1 or 4.2, the Company shall, subject to Sections 4.8 and 8.4, pay or distribute to such Member or to the legal representative of such Member, an amount in cash or, as determined by the Member Manager, in Securities (which may include short positions, as well as long positions) selected by the Member Manager or in cash and Securities selected by the Member Manager, equal in value to not less than 90 percent of the estimated Initial Withdrawal Amount (after taking into account the adjustments made pursuant to Sections 4.4 and 4.8). The 10 percent of the estimated Initial Withdrawal Amount held back is referred to as the *"Initial Reserve."*

(c)   On this same day, also known as the Final Withdrawal Day, the value of the remaining portion of the Membership Interest of the Member to be withdrawn, excluding the Initial Reserve, will be determined. This is the Final Withdrawal Amount.

(d)   If the amount sought to be withdrawn requires a computation that cannot be completed within such quarterly period or a delay is required in the opinion of the Member Manager in order to effectuate an orderly liquidation of a pro rata portion of the assets and/or investments of the Company, payment shall be made as soon thereafter as practicable.

(e)   On the last Business Day of the next calendar quarter following the Final Withdrawal Day pursuant to Sections 4.1 or 4.2, the Company will, subject to Sections 4.8 and 8.4, pay or distribute to such Member or his representative, an amount in cash and/or Securities (which may include short positions, as well as long positions) selected by the Member Manager, equal in value to not less than 90% of the estimated Final Withdrawal Amount (after taking into account the adjustments made pursuant to Sections 4.4 and 4.8). The 10 percent of the estimated Final Withdrawal Amount held back is referred to as the "*Final Reserve*."

(f)   Within thirty (30) days of completion and delivery to the Company of the annual financial audit for the Fiscal Year in which the Initial Withdrawal Day occurs, the Company will pay from the Initial Reserve to such Member or his representative, in cash and/or Securities (which may include short positions, as well as long positions) selected by the Member Manager, the amount of the excess, if any, of the Initial Withdrawal Amount of such Member determined finally upon completion of the audit over the amount previously paid in respect of the Initial Withdrawal Amount, or such Member or representative shall return and pay to the Company in cash the amount of the excess, if any, of the amount previously paid over such Initial Withdrawal Amount in each case without interest thereon. If the remainder is attributable to a Special Asset, the Member Manager may take the actions described in Section 12.3.[59]

(g)   Within thirty (30) days of completion and delivery to the Company of the annual financial audit for

---

[59] Within thirty days after completion and delivery of the audited financial statements for the Fiscal Year in which the Initial Withdrawal Day occurs, the Company will distribute the Initial Reserve to the Member following appropriate adjustments precipitated by the audit.

the Fiscal Year in which the Final Withdrawal Day occurs, the Company will pay from the Final Reserve to such Member or his representative, in cash and/or Securities (which may include short positions, as well as long positions) selected by the Member Manager, the amount of the excess, if any of the Final Withdrawal Amount of such Member determined finally upon completion of the audit over the amount previously paid in respect of the Final Withdrawal Amount, or such Member or representative shall return and pay to the Company in cash the amount of the excess, if any, of the amount previously paid in respect of the Final Withdrawal Amount over such Final Withdrawal Amount in each case without interest thereon. If the remainder is attributable to a Special Asset, the Member Manager may take the actions described in Section 12.3.[60]

(h)   The Company will not process third party payments. Withdrawal proceeds can only be remitted to an account in the registered Member's name.[61]

(i)   Notwithstanding any other provisions of this Agreement, the Member Manager may delay payment, in whole or in part, in respect of any withdrawal, if it determines that a portion of the withdrawal cannot be funded on the Withdrawal Day because a specific asset is a Special Asset, or otherwise has become part of a Designated

---

[60] The Final Reserve is computed and paid within thirty days of completion and delivery of the annual financial audit of the Fiscal Year in which the Final Withdrawal Day occurs. Again, the Final Reserve is subject to adjustment during the preparation of the final audit.

[61] Prohibiting third-party payments is a prudent requirement under the anti-money laundering rules.

Investment account. If a Member withdraws all or part of the Member's Membership Interest before the sale or other Disposition of a Designated Investment, instead of receiving the value at which the Designated Investment is recorded on the Company's books and records, the Withdrawing Member will maintain the Member's economic interest in the Designated Investment until the sale or other Disposition of such asset by the Master Fund and shall be considered a "Designated Investment Member" of the Company as described in Section 12.3(f).[62] The Designated Investment Member shall receive withdrawal payments on account of such Member's remaining Capital Account without regard to the Designated Investment. For as long as the withdrawing Designated Investment Member holds a Designated Investment, even if such Member has withdrawn all of the rest and remaining portion of the Member's Capital Account, the Member shall:

(i)   continue to receive the Member's allocable share of the gains, losses and expenses related solely to the Designated Investment; and

---

[62] Section 4.5(i) creates the ability of the Fund to designate certain assets as Special Assets or declare that they have become part of a Designated Investment account. These arrangements can also be called "side pockets." The important element of this arrangement is that a Withdrawing Member maintains that Member's economic interest in a Designated Investment until the sale or other disposition of the asset. In a Master feeder structure, the Master Fund holds the investment portfolio, and therefore the creation of side pockets occurs at the Master Fund level. The Feeder Fund's economic interest in those Special Assets needs to be accounted for up the chain from the Master Fund to the Feeder Fund. Because the Model Agreement is for a Fund that invests directly as well as through a Master Fund, this Agreement contains both Special Asset and Designated Investment mechanisms.

(ii)   remain a Member of the Company to the extent of the Member's interest in the Designated Investment.[63]

(j)   A Designated Investment Member will continue to be a Member until the Designated Investment Member has received all amounts payable with respect to all Designated Investments in the Member's Designated Investment account. Once the Designated Investment(s) has(ve) been disposed of, the Member will receive the Member's allocable share of the proceeds from the sale, less expenses, Management Fees and Performance Allocations related to such Designated Investment. Any amounts payable to a Designated Investment Member will be paid within thirty (30) Business Days following the total Disposition of the Designated Investment, at which point the Net Asset Value of the Company attributable to the Designated Investment should be known.

(k)   A *"Disposition"* of a Designated Investment includes a complete or partial disposition of a Designated Investment, or an earlier determination by the Investment Manager in its sole discretion that such Designated Investment has a readily ascertainable market value.[64]

(l)   The Company may delay part or all of the payments to Members requesting withdrawals if

---

[63] The practical impact of a Designated Investment account is that the Member must remain at risk with respect to the Member's share of the Designated Investment. If an asset has been so designated, it remains in the "corporate solution" of the Fund.

[64] Because assets can be designated as Special Assets for almost any purpose, including liquidity reasons and because they are hard to value.

the Company is unable to liquidate positions, there is a default or delay in payments due to the Company from banks, brokers or dealers or other entities, or other similar circumstances arise. The Company may also defer payment on withdrawals if raising the cash to pay such withdrawal would, in the Manager's good faith judgment, be unduly burdensome to the Company. The Company may also fund withdrawals either wholly or in part in cash or by in-kind Distribution of Securities or other property including interests in Side Pocket Accounts. The Fund will not pay interest to the withdrawing Member on any delayed or deferred payment and each Member acknowledges and agrees that the Member shall have no right to claim interest on any such payment.

(m)   The following two examples are intended to serve as theoretical and simplified examples regarding distributions upon withdrawals of capital from the Company and are meant as illustrations and not limitations or otherwise and do not limit the otherwise applicable discretion of the Member Manager under this Agreement in any fashion.

Example One.[65] Assume that a Member submits a Withdrawal Request for its entire Capital Account equal to $5 million on December 31, 2008.

---

[65] The inclusion of examples is purely a matter of drafting style. There is one school of thought that if the document has been properly drafted, the operation of the provision will be clear on its face and the application of the provision readily apparent. My personal view is that argument is hogwash. A good lawyer can impute ambiguity in almost any turn of phrase, and therefore clarity, especially in these complicated arrangements, is quite elusive. Moreover, agreements should not be a game of divining the original intent of the drafters. Investors are entitled to know with a fair degree of certainty what their rights and responsibilities are. To that end, I have found that examples tend to focus the reader in a way that straightforward

(continued...)

The Initial Withdrawal Day would be March 31, 2009. On such day, the Member would become a creditor of the Company with respect to $2.25 million, the Initial Withdrawal Amount less the Initial Reserve of $0.25 million. The Withdrawing Member would retain its interest equal to the remaining $2.75 million of the Withdrawal Amount; the $2.75 million investment would remain at risk in the Company and the Withdrawing Member's Capital Account will be allocated Net Profits and Net Losses and charged Management Fees and Performance Allocations until such time as such Member has been permitted to withdraw such Member's entire Capital Account.

On the last Business Day of the next calendar quarter following the Initial Withdrawal Day (June 30, 2009), the Company pays $2.25 million to the Withdrawing Member.

The Final Withdrawal Day would be June 30, 2009. On such day, the Member would become a creditor of the Company with respect to the value of the remaining portion of the Member's Capital Account less the Final Reserve of $0.25 million.

(continued...)

contract language cannot. The examples set forth at Section 4.5(m) are intended to make clear the timing of when notices must be delivered and when redemptions are actually paid and how much of those redemptions are paid on what day using what valuation date. If they are deleted from the actual operating agreement, they nevertheless should be retained and given to the administrator so that they are hard-wired by the administrator to reflect the proper operation of the Fund.

For simplicity's sake, the example assumes that the NAV has remained constant and on June 30, 2009, the Capital Account is worth $2.75 million.

On the last Business Day of the next calendar quarter following the Final Withdrawal Day (September 30, 2009), the Company pays $2.25 million to the Withdrawing Member.

Assume that the annual financial audit is completed 120 days after the end of the Fiscal Year ended June 30, 2009 (October 28, 2009). Within thirty (30) days of completion of the annual financial audit, or on or prior to November 27, 2009, the Company pays $0.5 million to the Withdrawing Member.

Example Two. Assume that a Member submits a Withdrawal Request for $5 million on March 31, 2009.

The Initial Withdrawal Day would be June 30, 2009. On such day, the Member would become a creditor of the Company with respect to $2.25 million, the Initial Withdrawal Amount less the Initial Reserve of $0.25 million. The Member would retain its interest equal to the remaining $2.75 million of the Withdrawal Amount; the $2.75 million investment would remain at risk in the Company and the Withdrawing Member's Capital Account will be allocated Net Profits and Net Losses and charged Management Fees and Performance Allocations until such time as such Member has been permitted to withdraw such Member's entire Capital Account.

On the last Business Day of the next calendar quarter following the Initial Withdrawal Day

(September 30, 2009), the Company pays $2.25 million to the Withdrawing Member.

Assume that the annual financial audit is completed 120 days after the end of the Fiscal Year ended June 30, 2009 (October 28, 2009). Within thirty (30) days of completion of the annual financial audit, or on or prior to November 27, 2009, the Company pays $0.25 million to the Withdrawing Member with respect to the Initial Withdrawal Amount.

The Final Withdrawal Day would be September 30, 2009. On such day, the Member would become a creditor of the Company with respect to the value of the remaining portion of the Member's Capital Account less the Final Reserve. For simplicity's sake, the example assumes that the NAV has remained constant and on September 30, 2009, the Capital Account is worth $2.75 million.

On the last Business Day of the next calendar quarter following the Final Withdrawal Day (December 31, 2009), the Company pays $2.25 million to the Withdrawing Member.

Assume that the annual financial audit is completed 120 days after the end of the Fiscal Year ended June 30, 2010 (October 28, 2010). Within thirty (30) days of completion of the annual financial audit, or on or prior to November 27, 2010, the Company pays the remaining $0.25 million to the Withdrawing Member.

4.6   Member Manager.[66]

(a)   The Member Manager shall have the right to withdraw all or a portion of its Capital Account and/or Management Fees or Performance Allocation at such times and in such amounts as the Member Manager, shall, in its sole discretion, determine, so long as such withdrawal does not adversely affect the tax status of the Company. For the avoidance of doubt, a withdrawal by the

---

[66] This is an innovation in the Model Agreement that allows the Member Manager essentially to withdraw its entire Capital Account without constituting a withdrawal or retirement of the Member Manager as the Member Manager of the Company. This provision is in reliance on a feature of Delaware law, which essentially states that any Member who has any interest in a limited liability company, including as a profits-only member, is a Member. It also attempts to avoid the trap for the unwary as Managers tend to want to withdraw their seed capital in order to start their next Fund. Being required to maintain significant assets in the Fund would limit that ability. Nevertheless, the marketplace tends to demand that managers "eat their own cooking" by having significant assets invested, so this usually ends up being an academic exercise. As this area of the tax law is still evolving, the reader must consult with tax counsel to see if there has been any determination on whether invested capital by the Manager is necessary to support the tax character of the performance Allocation.

Certain members of the tax bar suggest that not having capital at risk somehow changes the nature of the interest held by the Manager under the theory that a contribution "of property" is more important than a contribution of services. In its essence, this is a distinction without substance, as services under state law generally are a form of property insofar as they are transmuted into payment and such payment becomes property. Nevertheless, so long as these distinctions continue to exist as concerns, a Manager is well served to consult with his or her tax counsel to determine how much, if any, capital needs to be retained in its account in order to support treatment of the carried interest as a share of partnership profits.

If certain proposed legislation is successful (such legislation has been proposed from time to time that would eliminate the tax benefits of a carried interest; *see, e.g.,* H.R. 1935 proposed by Congressman Levin during 2009), then these distinctions would become irrelevant. The likelihood of any of these proposals being adopted is uncertain at this time, and so the manager should consult with his or her tax adviser concerning the advisability of maintaining assets in the account.

Member Manager of all of its Capital Account shall not constitute a withdrawal or retirement of the Member Manager as Member Manager of the Company. Such retirement must occur under Section 4.6(b).

(b)   The Member Manager may voluntarily withdraw and retire as Member Manager[67] of the Company at any time upon sixty (60) days' prior written notice to the Members. If the Member Manager has a Capital Account balance on the effective date of termination as Member Manager, that Capital Account will, at the election of the Company, be returned to the now-withdrawn Member Manager, or the Member Manager will become a Member as of such date, and the retired Member Manager will no longer be entitled to share in the Management Fee or Performance Allocation, unless the new Member Manager of the Company decides to share the Management Fee and/or Performance Allocation with the retired Member Manager.

(c)   In the event there is more than one Member Manager, the withdrawal and retirement of one or more Member Managers as Member Manager(s) of the Company, provided they are less than all of the Member Managers, shall not dissolve the Company. However, upon the withdrawal and retirement of all of the Member Managers as Member Manager(s) of the Company pursuant to Section 4.6(b) where no new Member Manager

---

[67] As a general matter of contract law, the Model Agreement does allow the Member Manager to voluntarily withdraw upon sixty days' prior written notice to the Members. It is the provision of such notice under Section 4.6(b) that actually triggers the retirement of the Member Manager under the Model Agreement.

has been appointed, the Company shall thereupon be dissolved in accordance with Section 11.1.

4.7   Costs of Withdrawal. In connection with any withdrawal, all expenses incurred by the Company related to such withdrawal, including but not limited to accounting, legal, arbitration and other professional fees and expenses, shall be borne by the Member who is withdrawing.

4.8   Limitations on Withdrawal. The payment of any Distribution under Section 4.1 may be based upon a reasonable estimate of the withdrawing Member's Capital Account and the adjustments provided under this Article 4 and Section 11.3(c), and the Fund may require a reserve for additional adjustments in the computation of the amount of the Distribution in consequence of such withdrawal, or may require a reserve pending the completion of a final determination of the amount to be distributed. The unused portion of any reserve shall be distributed after the Member Manager shall have determined that the need therefore shall have ceased. Any and all decisions regarding the amount and timing for the reserve shall be at the sole discretion of the Member Manager.

4.9   Withdrawals Coinciding with the Dissolution of the Company.[68] If any one or more of the events described in Section 11.1 occurs prior to the Distribution of the Withdrawal Amount pursuant to Section 4.5, the Member Manager may suspend action with respect to the withdrawal to which such Distribution relates until it is determined that a Liquidating Event has occurred or will occur. If a Liquidating Event is determined to have occurred, the determination and timing of Distributions from the Company shall be governed by Article 11 and the withdrawal will be deemed to not have occurred.

---

[68] Section 4.9 is a further innovation of the Model Agreement. This provision essentially forces the Fund under the liquidation provisions of Article 11 in the event that certain Liquidating Events described in Section 11.1 occur. The effect of this is to level the playing field among all investors who have pending notices of withdrawal and prevent bruising fights over the value of withdrawn interests by forcing all continuing investors at that time to be governed by one specific provision: the dissolution/liquidation provisions. Note: It is not a mere coincidence that the dissolution provisions appear at Article 11.

4.10   Suspension of Withdrawals.[69]

    (a)   The Member Manager may suspend the right of the Members of the Company to withdraw capital during any period when:

        (i)   any stock exchange or other exchange on which a significant portion of the assets and/or investments of the Master Fund or the Company are traded is closed, otherwise than for ordinary holidays, or dealings thereon are restricted or suspended;

        (ii)   there exists any state of affairs as a result of which (i) disposal of assets and/or investments of the Master Fund or the Company would not be reasonably practicable or cannot be completed in a timely fashion to meet withdrawal

---

[69] This is another innovation of the Model Agreement as the result of the turmoil of the 2008-2009 financial meltdown. Of course, the manager may add or delete from this litany of circumstances, and in a Fund that is a pure single-strategy Fund, references to the Master Fund would need to be deleted. The consequences of when a Fund suspends withdrawals are laid out in Section 4.10(b). It is important to note that in 4.10(b)(v), the Company may suspend valuation of assets and/or investments if withdrawals are suspended; and then again, it may not. The reason for this distinction is that a Fund may find itself in a position of holding valuable property, which, for one reason or another, but due to market forces, has impaired liquidity. If the Fund is prohibited from valuing assets, then arguably the Fund cannot pay Management Fees and the Fund would be unable to allow an angel investor to invest. If the Fund and the new investor agree on a valuation metric and on the value of the assets, the Manager should retain the right to accept such investments even though it has suspended withdrawals. And in order to prevent the appearance that a Manager has used new money to pay Withdrawing Investors, the withdrawal suspension can remain in effect even while the Fund continues to receive new assets. There is an expectation under these circumstances that all parties will act fairly, reasonably, and rationally, and that new investors will not invest if they are not comfortable with the transparency of the valuation of the underlying portfolio.

requirements and might seriously prejudice the Members of the Company or (ii) it is not reasonably practicable for the Master Fund or the Company fairly to determine the value of its net assets and/or investments;

(iii)   none of the Withdrawal Requests which have been made may be lawfully satisfied by the Company in dollars;

(iv)   there is a breakdown in the means of communication normally employed in determining the prices of a substantial part of the assets and/or investments of the Master Fund or the Company;

(v)   if the Member Manager determines, in its sole discretion, that such suspension is in the best interest of the Company;

(vi)   assets and/or investments of the Master Fund or the Company cannot be liquidated in a timely fashion to meet withdrawal requirements without having a significant adverse effect on the Master Fund or the Company; or

(vii)   redemptions from the Master Fund are suspended by the Master Fund.

(b)   No amounts may be withdrawn when withdrawals are suspended.

(i)   In such case, a Member may rescind its pending subscription agreement or Withdrawal Request, provided a request to rescind a subscription agreement or Withdrawal Request is actually received by the Member Manager before the suspension is terminated. In the event a Withdrawal Request is rescinded pursuant to the immediately preceding sentence, the Member rescinding its Withdrawal Request will not be charged a Revocation Fee. Unless withdrawn, subscription agreements and Withdrawal Requests will be acted upon on the first Investment Date or Withdrawal Date (as applicable) after the suspension is terminated.

(ii) Upon the determination by the Member Manager that any of the above-mentioned conditions no longer apply, withdrawal rights shall be promptly reinstated, and any pending Withdrawal Requests shall be honored in accordance with this Article 4.

(iii) The Company shall notify Members of any such suspension in such manner as it may deem appropriate.

(iv) The Company may, by written notice to any Members, suspend payment of withdrawal proceeds to such Members if the Member Manager reasonably deems it necessary to do so to comply with anti-money laundering laws and regulations applicable to the Company or any of the Company's service providers, or due to circumstances beyond its control, including but not limited to general civil disturbance or September 11, 2001 type events.

(v) The determination of the value of the assets and/or investments of the Company may be suspended when and if withdrawals are ever suspended.

ARTICLE 5
MANAGEMENT

5.1   Management.

(a)   The management of the Company shall be vested in a Member Manager. The Members hereby designate ABC Partners Inc. to be the sole Member Manager with full and exclusive right and control over the business affairs and investment activities of the Company. The Member Manager shall be authorized to act for the Company in every capacity under this Agreement and under the Act. [70]

(b)   The Member Manager may engage and compensate on behalf of the Company, from funds of the Company, and enter into joint ventures or employment, independent contractor, consultants or other agreements on such terms with such Persons, firms, Member Manager employees or corporations, including the Member Manager and any affiliated persons, related third parties or entities, as the Member Manager in its sole judgment shall deem advisable for the conduct and operation of the business of the Company.

(c)   In addition to any other rights and powers that the Member Manager may possess under this Agreement and applicable law, the Member Manager shall, except to the extent otherwise provided in this Agreement, have all specific rights and powers required or appropriate to its

---

[70] There can be only one captain of every ship, and in this case, Section 5.1(a) makes clear that the captain is the Member Manager who has sole and exclusive control over the business affairs and investment activities of the Fund.

management of the Company's business affairs and investment activities which, by the way of illustration but not by way of limitation, shall include the following rights and powers:

(i)   subject to the terms and conditions of this Agreement, to incur any and all expenditures which it considers to be necessary or advisable to the conduct of the Company's business;

(ii)   to establish the Company's investment objective, strategy, and restrictions;

(iii)   to direct the investment and trading activities of the Company;

(iv)   to invest and reinvest all of the Company's assets and/or investments in accordance with the objectives and strategies set forth in the Offering Memorandum;

(v)   to enter into, execute, amend, supplement, acknowledge and deliver any and all agreements, contracts, documents, certifications and instruments with such parties as the Member Manager deems necessary or advisable for the conduct of the Company's business;

(vi)   to maintain one or more clearing accounts, prime brokerage accounts (including margin accounts) or such other trading accounts, with brokers, clearing agents, futures commission merchants and other financial institutions, or to enter into arrangements to self-clear transactions with financial institutions such as Depository Trust Company or Euroclear;

(vii)   to retain accountants, consultants, experts, lawyers and brokers and other service providers on behalf of the Company;

(viii)   to pay, from the assets and/or investments of the Company, all debts and obligations incurred by the Company;

(ix)   to engage in any kind of activity and to perform and carry out contracts of any kind necessary or advisable to, or in connection with or convenient or incidental to, the accomplishment of the purposes of the Company;

(x)   to sell, assign, or otherwise dispose of all or substantially all of the assets and/or investments of the Fund on such terms and conditions as the Manager may determine;

(xi)   to enter into an agreement with such Persons as the Member Manager shall deem advisable, pursuant to which such Person shall provide office space, equipment, quotation services, back office and bookkeeping and other administrative services, along with traders, programmers, researchers and other professional services and the Member Manager is authorized to delegate to such Persons authority to make investment decisions for the account of the Company;

(xii)   to the extent permitted by applicable federal and state securities laws, to solicit the purchase of and sell Membership Interests in the Company to potential investors;

(xiii)   to borrow or loan money and property (including Securities), including the purchase of Securities on margin, either with or without collateral security, to mortgage, pledge, assign or otherwise hypothecate any one or more of the Company's properties, assets and/or investments to secure any such borrowing on behalf of the Company, including, without limitation, borrowings from a Member or an Affiliate thereof;

(xiv)   to incur and pay expenses and to establish reserves for estimated expenses and for unknown and unfixed liabilities and contingencies including but not limited to indemnification costs incurred to defend and indemnify against the claims of Members;

(xv)   to determine the Fair Value of any or all of the Company's Securities or other assets, investments or property, all of which valuations and determinations shall be final and binding on the Company and all Members;

(xvi)   to lease real and personal property;

(xvii)   to act as "tax matters partner" for the Company pursuant to Section 6231(a)(7) of the Code and to make or not make the election provided for in Section 754 of the Code;

(xviii)   to obtain insurance for the proper protection of the Company and its property and the Members; *provided, however,* that the Member Manager shall not be liable to the

Company or the Members for its failure to purchase any insurance or for the inadequacy of any coverage;

(xix)   to commence or defend any litigation involving the Company or the Member Manager in its capacity as the Member Manager, to retain legal counsel in connection therewith, and to have the Company pay any and all expenses, including attorneys' fees, incurred in connection therewith, and to settle or compromise claims by the Company against third parties and to compromise, settle or accept judgment with respect to claims against the Company;

(xx)   to the extent it is permissible to do so, to give any consents and to make, do and perform any acts, as may be required by the Advisers Act;[71]

---

[71] Section 5.1(c)(xx) should not be read as suggesting that a Member Manager can approve principal transactions prohibited by Section 206 of the Advisers Act. The SEC has repeatedly taken the position that Section 206 applies to all advisers, not just those that are registered under the Advisers Act. In a principal transaction, an adviser, acting as a principal for its own account, would knowingly sell a security to or purchase a security from a client (in this case, the Fund). Or, if the adviser has an affiliate that is a broker, such person knowingly effects the sale or purchase of a security for the account of such client out of a principal account of the broker. Such transactions are prohibited unless the Manager discloses to the Fund in writing before completion of the transaction the capacity in which the Manager is acting and obtains the consent of the Fund to such transaction. The question is whether a Manager who holds plenary authority over the Fund can consent on behalf of the investors or whether it is necessary for the adviser first to solicit the consent of the investors. Another approach that has been suggested is that the Manager can create an advisory committee or board populated by independent investors who will have the authority to approve such transactions. While the use of such an advisory committee or board makes logical sense, it has never been explicitly sanctioned by the regulatory authorities. The Member Manager is advised

(continued...)

(xxi) to appoint ABC Partners Inc., or such other entity as the Member Manager will determine from time to time in its sole discretion, to serve as the Investment Manager of the Company for purposes of providing investment advisory services (including, subject to the Member Manager's oversight, exercising the powers set forth in this Section) and certain administrative services to the Company;[72]

(xxii) to resolve, in its sole discretion, any ambiguity regarding the application of any provision of this Agreement in the manner it deems equitable, practicable and consistent with this Agreement and applicable law; provided that such resolution shall be reasonable and shall not discriminate unfairly against any Member;

(xxiii) to create one or more classes or series of voting and non-voting Membership Interests, with or without Allocation Layers, to, among other things, enable investors to

_____

(continued...)

to consult with competent Advisers Act counsel for assistance in any transaction that could be considered a principal transaction under the Advisers Act.

[72] Similarly, the Agreement gives the Member Manager the authority to appoint itself as the Investment Manager or such other entity as the Member Manager will determine. Of course, if this were a registered Fund, the appointment of a sub-adviser would require the consent of investors. The Member Manager is advised to consult with counsel to confirm that the appointment of any Investment Manager is consistent with the requirements of the Advisers Act and state law.

hold a class of Membership Interests that is non-voting;[73]

(xxiv)   to do any and all acts on behalf of the Company, and exercise all rights of the Company with respect to any interest in any Person, including, without limitation, the voting of Securities, participation in arrangements with creditors, the institution and settlement or compromise of suits and administrative proceedings and other like or similar matters; and

(xxv)   to take such other actions on behalf of the Company as it deems necessary or desirable to manage the business affairs and investment activities of the Company.

(d)   The investment objective and investment restrictions (each as described in the Offering Memorandum) may be amended from time to time by the Member Manager, provided that each Member is given prior notice and an opportunity to withdraw prior to the effective date of such

---

[73] The ability to create one or more classes or series of voting and non-voting Membership Interests is intended to allow the Investment Manager the flexibility to realize the full potential of the Agreement to protect investors and to protect the possibility of the Investment Manager earning a Performance Allocation. There is another possibility here, which is to enable the manager of a so-called 3(c)(1) Fund to create non-voting interests in order to attempt to fall within the exception to the look-through rules for purposes of counting whether the Fund has 100 or more persons as investors under Section 3(c)(1)(A). This is not a blank-check authority, as the jurisprudence interpreting Section 3(c)(1)(A) under the 1940 Act has created a series of substance over form and anti-abuse rules governing this interpretation. Again, the Manager is advised to seek counsel on how to implement the authorities set forth in subclause (xxiii).

amendments.[74] Any such withdrawal is not subject to the limitations set forth in Section 4.1 and the effective date of such withdrawal shall be determined by the Member Manager.

5.2   Other Business Interests of the Member Manager.

(a)   Nothing contained in this Agreement shall be deemed to preclude the Member Manager, the Investment Manager, the Liquidating Member, any Member or any beneficial owner, shareholder, Affiliate, trustee, officer, director, consultant, limited or general partner, member, employee, agent, attorney, representative and incorporator of any of the foregoing, their respective beneficial owners or partners, or any other Member or any consultant, agent, attorney, representative and incorporator of the Company (collectively, the *Affiliated Parties*) from engaging in or pursuing, directly or indirectly, any interest in other business ventures of any kind, nature or description, independently or with others, whether such ventures are competitive with the business of the Company or otherwise, including, without limitation, purchasing, selling or holding Securities

---

[74] Institutional investors with sophisticated investment allocation plans are particularly persnickety about "style drift." A manager that pursues returns, either by over-concentrating in one form of investment or moving out of the announced style, will quickly see their allocation reduced by an institutional investor. Nevertheless, the Model Agreement gives the Manager the authority to amend the investment objective and investment restrictions as described in the Offering Memorandum (such description is incorporated by reference by this clause) provided each Member is given prior notice and an opportunity to withdraw prior to the effective date of the amendment. The Model Agreement provides that such withdrawals are not subject to the limitations set forth in Section 4.1. Stated another way, every investor is entitled to know who his fiduciary is and how that fiduciary will manage the investor's money. This provision allows the Manager latitude but subjects the Manager to oversight and review.

for the account of any other Person or enterprise or for the Affiliated Party's own account, regardless of whether or not any such Securities are also purchased, sold or held for the account of the Company. Without limiting the foregoing, the Affiliated Parties shall be entitled to serve as the general partner of or manage any corporation, trust, portfolio or fund, limited liability company, partnership or account of any kind (each, an Account) and any such Account may engage in the same activities as the activities of the Company. In addition, the Affiliated Parties may act as investment adviser or investment manager for others, may manage funds, separate accounts or capital for others, may have, make and maintain investments in their own name or through other entities, and may serve as an officer, director, consultant, partner or stockholder of one or more investment funds, partnerships, securities firms or advisory firms. Neither the Company nor any Member shall have the right to participate in any manner in any such independent venture or other Account, however structured, or in any profits or income earned or derived by, or accruing to, the Affiliated Parties therefrom. The Member Manager's participation in any such venture or enterprise shall not be deemed a violation of its obligations hereunder or to the Company or the Members. The Member Manager/Investment Manager may purchase and sell interests in any entity affiliated with, or managed by, any Affiliated Party so long as such transaction is effected in accordance with applicable law.

(b)   Notwithstanding anything to the contrary herein, none of the Affiliated Parties shall have any obligation or responsibility to disclose or refer any particular investment or other opportunity of any kind whatsoever to the Company, even if such opportunity is of a character which, if presented to the Company, could be taken by the Company.

5.3   Binding Authority.[75] [76] The Member Manager shall have sole and exclusive power and authority to act for or bind the Company. Third parties dealing with the Company may rely conclusively upon any certification or representation by the Member Manager to the effect that it is acting on behalf of, for, or in the name of, the Company. The signature of the Member Manager shall be sufficient to bind the Company in any manner or on any agreement or document. Neither any Member (other than the Member Manager) nor the legal representative of any deceased, adjudicated incompetent or adjudicated bankrupt Member shall have any right to participate in the control of the business or affairs of the Company or any right or authority to act for or to bind the Company.[77]

5.4   Management Fee.

(a)   A monthly management fee (the *Management Fee*) payable to the Member Manager and/or its designee which may include the Investment

---

[75] Most Managers manage more than one investing vehicle or product. Limiting the Manager to one investment vehicle would dramatically reduce the earning capacity of the Manager. Section 5.2 is intended to make clear that while the Manager will provide to the Fund all attention that is due, the Manager is not precluded by the corporate opportunity doctrine, or otherwise, from managing other investment pools, separate accounts, and products. This also is designed to provide some type of protection to not only the Manager, but also to the Investment Manager, the Liquidating Member, and any other owner, officer, employee, etc., as such persons.

[76] The ABC Fund, LLC is not a general partnership; the Members of the Fund have no rights other than as set forth in the Agreement. The Member Manager is the captain of the ship.

[77] If the Manager chooses to create an advisory committee of Members or otherwise, it must make clear that the Advisory Committee does not have certain authorities less the Members of the Advisory Committee be required to register as investment advisor representatives. The advent of such committee would require modification of Section 5.3.

Manager shall be deducted from each Member's Capital Account equal to 0.125 percent (1.5 percent annualized)[78] multiplied by the value of such Capital Account on the calculation day. The Management Fee is paid monthly in arrears,[79] based on the value of each Member's Capital Account as of the last Business Day of each calendar month (or upon the occurrence of a Liquidating Event or the date of Termination, in each case, if such date is other than the end of a calendar month). The Management Fee will be computed before the application of the Performance Allocation and all expenses other than the Management Fee shall be taken into consideration when calculating the value of the Capital Accounts upon which such fees are based. Management Fees also will be charged on all amounts withdrawn before payment of such withdrawal. New subscriptions will accrue Management Fees as of the first day of the calendar month in which the Company's acceptance of the subscription is to be effective. The Company will pay the Management Fee in dollars promptly after the last Business Day of each calendar month. The Management Fee will be prorated for any period that is less than a full

---

[78] This rate in a Model Agreement (1.5 percent annualized) is neither high nor low. Fees range from a low of fifty basis points to a high of 300 basis points. Fees at either end of the range are rare.

[79] The Member Manager of the Fund is a Registered Investment Adviser. Registered Investment Advisers may not accept fees in advance without potentially being required to rebate fees and meeting other requirements under the Advisers Act. A fee paid in arrears is consistent with registered adviser practice.

calendar month.[80] To the extent the Management Fee is paid at the Company level, the Company will not be charged a management fee at the Master Fund level.[81] The Member Manager, in its sole discretion, and without notice to or consent of the other Members, may waive or reduce the Management Fee with respect to any Member and may cause all or a portion of the Management Fee to be paid to another party, including one of its Affiliates, any sub-adviser and/or any placement agent.[82]

(b)   For each Fiscal Period, the Management Fee shall be specially allocated to the Members in accordance with Section 5.4.[83] The Management Fee allocated to a Member shall be allocated among such Member's Allocation Layers in

---

[80] Management Fees are a function of time, and therefore Management Fees are prorated for any period less than a full calendar month. In contrast, Performance Fees or Allocations are never prorated based on time.

[81] In a Master Feeder Fund structure, the incidence of the Management Fee can occur at either level. Ordinarily it occurs at the Master Fund level if it is unlikely that there will be any accommodation of the Management Fee for individual investors. The Management Fee is simply charged as an expense of the overall operation of the business and reduces the assets contained in the Master Fund. In this instance, the Model Agreement allows the Investment Manager and Manager to reduce the Management Fee in side letter arrangements, or, perhaps, share the Management Fee with private placement brokers. For that reason, it is being paid at the Feeder Fund level.

[82] The Manager must retain the ability to share the Management Fee with a Subadvisor. Any possible fee waivers or reimbursements should be shared on the same basis that the Manager and the Investment Manager/Sub-Adviser share the Management Fee.

[83] Because the Management Fee can be different for different investors, it is allocated to the Members specially.

proportion to their respective Allocation Layer Percentages.

5.5   Fees and Expenses.

(a)   The Company shall pay all of its own operating expenses that are not borne by the Master Fund. Operating expenses include (but are not limited to): fees paid to the Member Manager and the Investment Manager; fees paid to the Administrator (including for middle and back office services) and the Accounting Agent; interest on margin accounts and other indebtedness; legal, compliance, audit, and accounting fees and expenses (including third party accounting services); Organizational and Start-up Expenses; borrowing charges on Securities sold short[84]; insurance premiums; regulatory filing fees and custodial fees; fees and expenses of consultants and advisers; distribution expenses, including, Blue Sky costs[85], if any; fees for bookkeeping, record keeping, auditing, tax preparation and other similar services relating to the affairs of the Company, and as may be incurred by the Member Manager and the Investment Manager with respect to the affairs of the Company; investment expenses such as commissions, contract fees[86], research fees and expenses (including research-

---

[84] Generally, expenses for the purchase and sale of securities are rolled into the basis of the security sold/purchased and are not separately stated.

[85] Some states (notably New York) require registration BEFORE any sales activity. Most states allow a period of time to elapse before a fun is required to register under the Blue Sky rules; some states have *de minimis* exceptions, and others have so-called self-executing exceptions.

[86] These apply in certain futures and forward trades. *See* footnote 84.

related travel expenses incurred in researching potential investment opportunities); salaries and benefits of personnel hired by the Company on a full or part time basis[87]; costs associated with pricing services and valuation experts; costs associated with select news, quotation and similar information services; and any other expenses reasonably related to the purchase, sale or transmittal of Company assets and/or investments. Included in these fees and expenses payable by the Company may be amounts charged by ABC Partners Inc. for certain legal, consulting and administrative services it provides to the Company and the Master Fund through employees of ABC Partners Inc.[88]

(b)   Organizational expenses, start-up expenses and offering expenses shall be borne or reimbursed by the Company. The Member Manager and the Investment Manager shall be entitled to obtain reimbursement from the Company for all such costs and expenses borne by either or both of them on behalf of the Company (specifically including Organizational, Start-up and offering expenses which may have been incurred prior or

---

[87] This is a prophylactic measure, added just in case a regulator requires the Fund to hire its own chief compliance officer or other professional staff. Also, the traditional form of having a third-party entity act as the manager or investment adviser to the fund is not a absolute requirement. The Fund could hire its own professional staff as employees. This is common in certain family office situations. It would also be useful if the fund wanted to meet the requirements of a state law economic stimulus program, such as the Pennsylvania Keystone Opportunity Zone program, that requires the Fund to actually have a business tax nexus to qualify for certain economic development incentives.

[88] Inter-company allocations of common/shared expenses present thorny business problems. It generally is better to use a "bright-line allocation rule" such as a top-line/gross revenue allocation.

subsequent to the date hereof) on the subscription date where cumulative subscriptions received and accepted by the Master Fund exceed $5 million.[89] In accordance with GAAP, such costs shall be treated as an expense when incurred. For federal tax purposes, to the extent funds are spent, the Company may take an immediate $5,000 deduction for its Organizational Expenses and amortize the remainder of its Organizational Expenses over one hundred eighty (180) months, and take an immediate $5,000 deduction for its Start-up Expenses and amortize the remainder of its applicable Start-up Expenses over one hundred eighty (180) months beginning with the month in which the Company begins business, but only to the extent such expenses are not otherwise classified as "Syndication Expenses" pursuant to Treas. Reg. § 1.709-2(b). These first year deductions will be reduced by the amount that total Organizational Expenses and Start-up Expenses respectively and separately each exceed $50,000.

(c)   The Investment Manager shall pay expenses, such as salaries and benefits of personnel of the Investment Manager assigned to the Company, costs associated with office space, telephone, utilities and computer equipment/support, and costs associated with news, quotation and similar information and systems provided by the Investment Manager. The Investment Manager, in its sole discretion may liquidate assets and/or

---

[89] Including a minimum Fund asset size as a perquisite to reimbursement for expenses is purely a business decision. If the Manager and promoter intend to seek first dollar reimbursement, it should consider whether an expense cap makes sense, so as not to hurt Fund performance in the early years of the fund.

investments held by the Company to pay Management Fees, Performance Allocations and other costs and expenses incurred by or on behalf of the Company.[90]

(d)   Any and all expenses of the Company stated in Section (a) and (b) may, but not necessarily will, be paid at the Master Fund level. If the payment is made at the Master Fund level, such payment arrangements are merely an accommodation to the Company; and such expenses remain the expenses of the Company for tax and accounting purposes, insofar as the Master Fund is acting merely as a paying agent on its behalf. Notwithstanding the above, expenses incurred by the Master Fund relating to (i) portfolio management; (ii) hedging and trading expenses; (iii) portfolio administration and valuation; (iv) portfolio auditing expenses; (v) custodian expenses; (vi) tax preparation and legal expenses; and (vii) Cayman Islands registration fee and other expenses related to the affairs of the Master Fund shall remain the expenses of the Master Fund and will not be allocated to the Company.

(e)   In the event the auditors, tax preparation firms or any other service providers charge an aggregate fee at the Master Fund level for the services provided to the Master Fund, the Company and any other feeder fund (collectively, the *Funds*; the

---

[90] This is an often overlooked but essential provision to include in the Operating Agreement. After all, the Manager is in the business of managing money for a fee and a share of the profits. If it can't be paid currently with little fanfare, it will have difficulty retaining qualified staff. While it is often suggested that analysts and staff should "work on the come," and share in the rewards when the business success is realized, Fund promoters should be realistic; qualified staff will not work for free, especially in a start-up context.

Company and the other feeder funds are referred to as the *Feeder Fund(s)*), such fees will be allocated on a per dollar basis based on the ratio of the Net Asset Value of each Fund including the Master Fund, to the sum of the Net Asset Values of all Funds including the Master Fund. Notwithstanding the above, any special charges related to a specific Feeder Fund will be allocated to that Feeder Fund.

(f)   Appropriate reserves may be created for contingent liabilities, if any, as of the date any such contingent liability becomes known to the Member Manager. Such reserves shall reduce the Net Asset Value of the Company for all purposes, including withdrawals.

5.6   <u>Agents and Consultants</u>. The Member Manager shall be authorized to retain agents of and consultants to the Company. The Member Manager shall not be liable for the acts or omissions of such agents of or consultants to the Company.

5.7   <u>Concurrent Status</u>. A Member may at the same time be both a Member Manager and a Member, in which event its, his or her rights and obligations in each such capacity shall be determined separately in accordance with the provisions hereof and of the Act.[91]

---

[91] This provision is designed to allow a Manager an argument that its activities can be compartmentalized, and that the forms of the Manager's interest and investment should be separately respected. Managers with significant investment in the Fund should assiduously avoid using such investment in a manner that suggests it is not just a passive investment. Structured finance vehicles traditionally disenfranchised shares/interests held by the Manager because of the conflict of interest such investments by the Manager create. Hedge fund practice has embraced the opposite approach: most investors want assurances that the Manager has a significant investment at risk in the Fund (i.e., they want the Manager to "eat his own cooking"). Managers need to be aware of the risks that this poses as well as the likelihood that investors will expect the Manager to allow his or her investment to

(continued...)

5.8   Indemnification. The Company shall indemnify, defend and hold harmless (i) the Affiliated Parties; (ii) trustees of any of the foregoing; (iii) controlling persons of any of the foregoing; (iv) successors, assigns and personal representatives of any of the foregoing, and (v) any other Person who serves at the request of the Member Manager on behalf of the Company as a partner, member, officer, director, employee, attorney or agent of any other Person (and each of their respective heirs and legal and personal representatives) (collectively, the *Indemnified Parties*), to the fullest extent permitted by law, from and against any loss (including a trading error loss)[92], damage, liability (including, without limitation, tax liabilities, and interest and penalties associated therewith), cost or expense (including, without limitation, judgments, fines, amounts paid or to be paid in settlement and attorneys' fees and expenses)[93] arising out of or in connection with (a) any act or failure to act or alleged act or failure to act by an Indemnified Party arising out of, in connection with or in any way related to the Company or (b) the affairs of the Company; except that the Company shall not indemnify any Indemnified Party for any loss, damage,

---

(continued...)

be the "last dollar in." This is a business risk for the Manager that needs to be addressed in the legal documents.

[92] Trading error losses can be significant. The issue always is even if a trading error is recognized, how, if at all, should the Manager make the Fund whole and for what amount. If a significant amount of time passed between when the error was recognized and when it was corrected, the underlying position may have moved up AND down during that time. Also, should the value of the alternative position be used as an offset? And should the amount to be corrected be measured as of the last statement date, the discovery date, or the reinvestment date? This provision attempts to side-step the issue altogether by making it clear that the trading loss is the Fund's, and hence all of the investors' loss, and the Manager will not participate in that loss (other than perhaps if the Manager is also an investor). Any claim against the Manager or the other persons to be indemnified will be immediately met with a demand for indemnification from the Fund.

[93] The indemnification is plenary: fines, taxes, interest, and penalties...any claim for damages is covered, save if the claim is for a violation of the federal securities laws, then the indemnity must yield. *See* text accompanying footnote 95.

liability, cost or expense (x) arising from the willful misconduct, gross negligence, fraud or bad faith of such Indemnified Party[94], (y) as to which indemnification is barred under the federal securities laws, the Act, or other applicable laws, or (z) if applicable, as to the Indemnified Party's share as a Member in any losses or expenses of the Company. Notwithstanding the above, indemnification shall not exceed the maximum level permitted under applicable federal, state or other laws and any indemnification or hold harmless arrangement shall not be deemed to waive and shall not waive any non-waivable rights that an investor may have under applicable federal or state law.[95] Such attorneys' fees and expenses shall be paid by the Company as they are incurred upon receipt of an undertaking by or on behalf of the Indemnified Party to repay such amounts if it is ultimately determined by a court or other tribunal that such Indemnified Party is not entitled to indemnification with respect thereto.

5.9   <u>Exculpation.</u>

(a)   None of the Indemnified Parties shall be liable, responsible or accountable in damages or otherwise to the Company or to any Member for any act or failure to act pursuant to this Agreement or otherwise, except where such act or failure to act constitutes willful misconduct, gross negligence, fraud or bad faith. The Member Manager and such other persons shall be entitled to rely upon the opinion or the advice of counsel, public accountants or other experts experienced in the matter(s) at issue; such an opinion or such advice shall afford full protection for the Member Manager and such other Persons with respect to any act or failure to act by the Member Manager

---

[94] "…willful misconduct, gross negligence, fraud, or bad faith of such Indemnified Party…": fairly standard carve-out.

[95] This is the current no-action position of the Securities and Exchange Commission. *Heitman Capital Management LLC, et al*, SEC No Action Letter, File No. 801-15473 (February 12, 2007).

or such other Persons in good faith reliance on such an opinion or on such advice; and such an act or failure to act shall in no event subject the Member Manager or any such other person to liability to the Company or any other Member.

(b)   The Member Manager shall not be personally liable for the return of any Member's Capital Contributions or any additions to any Member's Capital Account or any portion thereof. [96]

(c)   Notwithstanding any provision of this Agreement to the contrary, none of the Indemnified Parties shall be liable to the Company or any Member for indirect, special, consequential or punitive damages or losses of any kind whatsoever (including but not limited to lost profits), whether or not foreseeable and regardless of whether the claim for loss or damage is made in negligence, for breach of contract or otherwise. [97]

5.10   The Investment Manager.

(a)   ABC Partners Inc. is additionally the Investment Manager of the Company. Should at any time ABC Partners Inc. choose not to serve as the investment manager of the Company or be removed as Investment Manager by the Member

---

[96] There is no deficit make-up provision. The assets of the Fund represent a "zero-sum game."

[97] While the limitation on so-called expectancy damages is well established in American jurisprudence (and is one of the first cases studied by first-year law students in Torts), the desire of investors to be made whole from their investment losses—and lawyers to try to get them that result—often trumps training. This provision makes clear that "lost profit" is the responsibility of the investor. The investor's remedy—absent fraud—remains withdrawal.

Manager, the Member Manager may delegate any part or all of its investment management authority under this Agreement to another investment manager which may be an Affiliate of the Investment Manager, or of the Member Manager, for the provision of investment management services, including but not limited to entering into an agreement on behalf of the Company with other service providers for the provision of certain recordkeeping, accounting and administrative services; provided, however, that the Member Manager shall retain responsibility to the Members for the management and conduct of the activities of the Company and may remove the Investment Manager at any time.

(b)   Any agreement delegating any part of the investment management authority of the Member Manager or the Investment Manager to another investment manager will (i) be in writing, executed by the Company, the Member Manager and the Investment Manager (ii) specify the authority so delegated, and (iii) expressly require that such delegated authority be exercised by the Investment Manager in conformity with the terms and conditions of such delegation agreement and this Agreement.

5.11   Assets. Any asset owned by the Company may be registered in the name of the Company, or in the name of a nominee, or in a "street name."[98] Any corporation, brokerage firm or transfer agent called upon to

---

[98] Almost every security needs to be held in street name as they are traded in dematerialized form through the Depository Trust Company. This does post some modicum of risk in that the broker might be unable to meet demands from all clients to return their funds. The recent high-profile bankruptcy of Lehman Brothers Inc. merely resulted in the transfer of the brokerage accounts to another broker. *See generally*, Rule 15c3-3 under the Securities Exchange Act of 1934, as

(continued...)

transfer any assets and/or investments to or from the name of the Company shall be entitled to rely upon instructions or assignments signed or purporting to be signed by the Member Manager or its agent without inquiry as to the authority of the Person signing or purporting to sign such instructions or assignments or as to the validity of any transfer to or from the name of the Company; provided, however, that any corporation, brokerage firm or transfer agent holding cash or other assets and/or investments of the Company shall be expected to comply with any special instructions concerning payment and delivery given to it in writing by the Member Manager.

5.12   Limitations on Powers of the Member Manager. The Member Manager shall not have the authority without the written approval of all of the Members to:

(a)   do any act in contravention of the Certificate of Formation or this Agreement;

(b)   do any act which would make it impossible to carry on the ordinary business of the Company, other than to dissolve the Company pursuant to Article 11 hereof;

(c)   confess a material judgment against the Company, although the Member Manager may settle suits or claims against the Company where the Member Manager determines, in the Member Manager's sole discretion, that settlement is in the best interests of the Company and such settlement may include a confession of judgment clause; [99]or

---

(continued...)

amended, for a discussion of the custody and reserve rules applicable to broker dealers.

[99] Confession of judgment is an ancient procedure that allows parties to a commercial dispute to agree within the contract that one or the other or both

(continued...)

(d)   possess Company property or assign rights to specific Company property for other than a Company purpose.[100]

5.13   Additional Rights of the Member Manager.

(a)   In addition to the right and power of the Member Manager to manage the Company as provided herein or granted or implied by law, the Member Manager shall have the right, on behalf of the Company, to execute and file any and all reports, schedules, notices and other instruments or documents required to be filed by the Company under any applicable federal or state law, rule or regulation, or deemed, in the judgment of the Member Manager, to be necessary or appropriate under the circumstances. Subject to any restrictions imposed by law, each Member agrees to furnish promptly upon request any information concerning such Member and its Affiliates as the Member Manager reasonably believes necessary or

---

(continued...)

parties will not contest liability under the contract. Under this procedure, the party who is the beneficiary of the confession of judgment can go to the clerk of the court or prothonotary who will enter a judgment for the beneficiary without the cost, expense, and delay associated with a trial. The party immediately proceeds to collection. This is a valuable collection technique where there are unlikely to be any defenses to the liability. The prohibition is intended to prevent the Manager from assuming a third party's liability and confessing it against the Fund. However, the Manager can settle legitimate disputes, and such settlement may even include a confession of judgment as a payment mechanism.

[100] This is an obvious prohibition against embezzlement. Conversion to the Manager's own purposes is prohibited. But note that the Manager can possess such property momentarily for the Company's purposes. The Manager will need to contend with the SEC custody rules that limit holding customer funds without certain safeguards and protections being in place.

desirable in order to comply with filing requirements arising under applicable laws, rules and regulations; and the Member Manager is authorized to disclose such information concerning each Member as it determines, in its sole discretion, is required under the circumstances. Each Member agrees that, at the request of the Member Manager, it will keep current any such information previously furnished and that the Member Manager may rely on the accuracy and current status of such information in making any filing on behalf of the Company.[101]

(b) If reasonably required to comply with any applicable law, rule or regulation, each Member agrees to disclose to the Member Manager, upon request, its holdings and the holdings of any of such Member's Affiliates of all securities and other obligations of the issuer or obligor of any specified Securities that the Company owns or intends to acquire (and, unless otherwise prohibited pursuant to the provisions of a confidentiality agreement or otherwise, such other information relative thereto as may be so requested). Requests for information by the Member Manager hereunder shall indicate the basis for the request and the purpose for which the information is sought. All responses shall be provided expeditiously on a time-is-of-the-essence basis.

---

[101] This provision is intended to enable the Manager to get all information necessary for the Manager to comply with FINRA's New Issue rules that periodically require the Fund to certify its eligibility to participate in New Issues. This provision also enables the Fund to collect and turn over information under any jurisdiction's anti-money laundering rules, and similar anti-abuse regimens.

(c)   Each Member acknowledges that the Member Manager/Investment Manager also manages collective trust funds, separate accounts, investment funds and other pooled investment vehicles and accounts. As a result, the Members authorize the Member Manager to reconcile conflicts of interest in trading, investing and sale of Securities as the Member Manager sees fit consistent with the Member Manager's overriding responsibilities under applicable law, including, without limitation, the Advisers Act, the Investment Company Act, the Advisers Act Rules and the FINRA/NASD Rules. Members further acknowledge that such reconciliation may adversely affect the Company and the Members and agree to hold the Member Manager harmless with respect to such actions provided that the Member Manager acts in good faith. [102]

5.14   Soft Dollar Arrangements.

(a)   The Investment Manager is authorized to determine the broker or dealer to be used for each securities transaction for the Master Fund or the Company. In selecting brokers or dealers to execute transactions, the Investment Manager need not solicit competitive bids and does not

---

[102] Correlative duties to different clients will cause conflicts of interest to arise. The Manager needs a way to deal with them without subjecting itself to unreasonable cost and expense. In an investment management version of the "Theory of Relativity," conflicts must be assessed from all points of view—incumbent short provisions can have priority over to-be-acquired long positions in long-only accounts. Such decisions are made in real time, and the Manager should not be second-guessed for decisions made in good faith.

have an obligation to seek the lowest available commission cost.[103]

(b)   Except for services that would be a Master Fund or Company expense or as otherwise described below, the Investment Manager will use its best efforts, but is not obligated, to limit the use of "soft dollars" to obtain research and brokerage services to services which constitute research and brokerage within the meaning of Section 28(e) of the Securities Exchange Act of 1934, as amended.[104] Research services within the Section 28(e) safe harbor may include, but are not limited to, research reports (including market research); certain financial newsletters and trade journals; software providing analysis of securities portfolios; corporate governance research and rating services; attendance at certain seminars and conferences; discussions with research analysts; meetings with corporate executives; consultants'

---

[103] Cheaper is not always better. "Best execution" is a better gauge for measuring the performance of the Fund's brokerage. If an affiliated broker is used for some or all of the trades, the Manager needs to take appropriate steps to avoid principal trades and comply with all record-keeping requirements.

[104] Recent SEC action has virtually eliminated the soft dollar abuses that had cropped up in recent years. Soft dollars are, in effect, a purchase price adjustment—in exchange for an order bearing a commission priced at a few pennies per share traded, the broker executing the trade would give the investor rebates in the form of research. The rebates expanded over the years to include computer systems, software, trips, etc. When the research was used by the Manager in its investment management business, an argument arose that the Manager's other accounts were being unfairly benefited. The Manager's defense was that all accounts trade; and so eventually all such benefits evened out. However, with certain accounts being actively traded and others possibly in a buy and hold mode, the "all will come out in the wash" approach limped. Congress responded with a safe harbor (Section 28(e)) that alleviated the concern while at the same time endorsing certain soft dollar barter practices. The SEC's interpretation limits this to actual research and other specified costs.

advice on portfolio strategy; data services (including services providing market data, company financial data and economic data); advice from brokers on order execution; and certain proxy services. Brokerage services within Section 28(e) may include, but are not limited to, services related to the execution, clearing and settlement of securities transactions and functions incidental thereto (i.e., connectivity services between an investment manager and a broker-dealer and other relevant parties such as custodians); trading software operated by a broker-dealer to route orders; software that provides algorithmic trading strategies; software used to transmit orders; clearance and settlement in connection with a trade; electronic communication of allocation instructions; routing settlement instructions; post trade matching of trade information; and services required by the Securities and Exchange Commission or a self regulatory organization such as comparison services, electronic confirms or trade affirmations.

(c)   The Investment Manager will allocate, in good faith, the relative proportion of a product or service used to assist the Investment Manager in carrying out its investment decision-making responsibilities and the relative proportion used for administrative or other purposes outside of Section 28(e). The proportion of the product or service attributable to assisting the Investment Manager in carrying out its investment decision-making responsibilities will be paid through brokerage commissions generated by client transactions and the proportion attributable to administrative or other purposes outside of Section 28(e) will be paid for by the Investment Manager from its own resources.

(d)   The Members acknowledge that research and brokerage services obtained by the use of commissions arising from the Master Fund's portfolio transactions may be used by the Investment Manager in its other investment activities and thus, the Master Fund may not necessarily, in any particular instance, be the direct or indirect beneficiary of the research or brokerage services provided.[105]

(e)   The Members acknowledge that although the Investment Manager will make a good faith determination that the amount of commissions paid is reasonable in light of the products or services provided by a broker, commission rates are generally negotiable and thus, selecting brokers on the basis of considerations that are not limited to the applicable commission rates may result in higher transaction costs than would otherwise be obtainable. The Investment Manager's receipt of such products or services and the determination of the appropriate allocation in the case of "mixed use" products or services create a potential conflict of interest between the Investment Manager and its clients, which the Members acknowledge and waive.

(f)   In selecting brokers and negotiating commission rates, the Investment Manager will take into account the financial stability and reputation of brokerage firms, and the research, brokerage or other services provided by such brokers. The Investment Manager may place transactions with a broker or dealer that (i) provides the Investment Manager (or an affiliate) with the opportunity to

---

[105] *See* footnote 104.

participate in capital introduction events sponsored by the broker-dealer or (ii) refers investors to the Company or other products advised by the Investment Manager (or an affiliate), if otherwise consistent with seeking best execution; provided the Investment Manager is not selecting the broker dealer in recognition of the opportunity to participate in such capital introduction events or the referral of investors.[106]

(g)   The Investment Manager may, but is not required, to aggregate client orders to achieve more efficient execution or to provide for equitable treatment among accounts managed by the Investment Manager, including the Master Fund and the Company. Members acknowledge and consent to procedures whereby clients participating in aggregated trades will be allocated securities based on the average price achieved for such trades.

(h)   The Investment Manager is authorized hereby to hire separate independent trading firms in order to obtain better prices and/or execution, and such trading firms will be paid through additional commissions to be borne by the Company.

5.15   Good Faith Time and Attention of the Member Manager. The Member Manager and its trustees, officers, directors, consultants, agents, and employees shall devote such time to the Company and its objectives, purposes and powers as shall be reasonably necessary in the opinion of the Member Manager to achieve the objectives of the Company. The Member Manager shall perform its obligations under this Agreement to the best of

---

[106] Capital introductions are not a part of soft dollars, but they are essential to growing the fund. Growing the fund reduces allocable expense on a per-share basis and allows the Fund a bigger footprint in New Issues and other instances where having a certain fund size is essential to participation.

its ability, and the Member Manager shall use reasonable efforts to carry out the objectives, purposes, and powers of the Company for the benefit of all of the Members. The Member Manager, however, is required to devote to the Company only that amount of time and attention that the Member Manager in its sole discretion deems reasonably necessary to achieve the Company's objectives.

5.16   Termination and Replacement of Member Manager.[107]

(a)   The Member Manager may only be terminated from the position of Member Manager by an affirmative vote of a Required Interest of Members, and may only resign from such position, upon sixty days' prior written notice of termination or resignation, as applicable.

(b)   In the event of termination of the Member Manager by the Members, the Company shall have all of the rights and remedies available with respect thereto at law or equity. On and after the receipt by the Member Manager of written notice of termination, and upon expiration of the sixty-day notice period specified in Section 5.16(a), or the appointment of, and the acceptance of the appointment by a successor Member Manager, if earlier, all authority and power of the Member Manager in its capacity as such under this Agreement shall automatically and without further action by any Person or entity pass to and be vested in the successor Member Manager or the Fund will be liquidated in accordance with Article

---

[107] The ability to remove the Member Manager and appoint a replacement will likely cause the interests in the Fund that participate in the process to be considered "voting securities" for purposes of Section 3(c)(1) of the 1940 Act. If an entity holds 10 percent or more of the voting securities of the Fund, the Fund will need to count the number of investors in that entity for purposes of determining if the Fund has 100 or fewer beneficial owners.

11 if no successor Member Manager has been appointed. Upon written request from a Required Interest of Members, the Member Manager shall deliver to the Company all property and documents of the Company or copies of documents otherwise relating to the Securities or other assets and/or investments of the Company then in the custody of the Member Manager. Management Fees and Performance Allocations due to the Member Manager will be prorated to the date of termination.

5.17   Advisers Act Assignment. Notwithstanding anything to the contrary contained herein, if at any time the Member Manager shall be registered as an investment adviser pursuant to the provisions of the Advisers Act, then any act or occurrence under Article 9 hereof which, in the opinion of counsel to the Company, constitutes an "assignment" of an investment advisory contract by the Member Manager for purposes of the Advisers Act shall be deemed to be of no force or effect without the consent to such "assignment" of a Majority in Interest of the Members. Such consent may be obtained through a negative consent procedure that requires the Member to object after the receipt of written notice within 60 days, but if no such objection is received, the Member's consent will be presumed.[108]

---

[108] Few rules cause more consternation than the prohibitions on assignment of adviser contracts. While an adviser should be able to realize on the enterprise value of its business, the law requires that an investor always know the identity of the fiduciary managing the investor's money. This conflict has been translated into a prohibition on assignment without consent. The question is the form of consent: Can consent be presumed after appropriate notice, or must it be affirmative? Clearly, the gold standard is affirmative consent, but in appropriate circumstances, a negative consent procedure may be appropriate. Consult with your securities counsel.

ARTICLE 6
CAPITAL CONTRIBUTIONS

6.1   Initial Capital Contributions.

   (a)   Each Member has or shall pay to the Company
          the aggregate amount of such Member's Capital
          Contribution in the form specified in Section 6.5.
          Such contribution shall be credited to the Capital
          Account of each such Member in accordance with
          Section 7.1(d).

   (b)   The Member Manager shall maintain a sufficient
          investment in the Company to ensure that the
          Company will be treated as a partnership for U.S.
          federal income tax purposes. The Member
          Manager shall make this determination in its sole
          discretion.[109]

   (c)   The minimum initial Capital Contribution of a
          Member (other than the Member Manager) shall
          be $1 million; except that the Member Manager
          may, in its sole discretion, permit any Member to
          make an initial Capital Contribution of less than
          $1 million upon such terms and conditions, if any,
          as the Member Manager may deem appropriate;
          and further except, that the Member Manager may
          increase the minimum initial Capital Contribution
          for new Members to any amount greater than $1
          million in its sole discretion and from time to time
          and without the consent of any Member.
          Employees of the Investment Manager and its

---

[109] If the Fund has only the Member Manager as a Member and one other Member,
it is imperative that the Member Manager maintain its interest to avoid the Fund
losing its status as a partnership for federal tax purposes. *See also* Sections 4.6 and
6.2.

Affiliates who become Members will not be required to meet the minimum Capital Contribution requirement.[110]

6.2   Additional Contributions by the Member Manager. The Member Manager, in its capacity as a Member, may make Capital Contributions to the capital of the Company at such times and in such amounts as the Member Manager may, in its sole discretion, determine (and, in accordance with Section 4.6, may withdraw all or a portion of its Capital Account). These contributions shall be credited to the Capital Account of the Member Manager in accordance with Section 7.1(d)(i).

6.3   Additional Contributions by the Members.

(a)   The Member Manager may, in its sole discretion, and without any consent or action by any other Member, accept additional contributions to the capital of the Company in the minimum amount of $100,000 from any Member as of (i.e., immediately preceding) the start of business on the first Business Day of any Fiscal Period (on a more or less frequent basis, at the discretion of the Member Manager). [111] Subject to the right of the Member Manager to accept Capital Contributions at other times, each additional Capital Contribution contributed by a Member shall be attributable to a specific Allocation Layer for purposes of determining the Performance Allocations.

---

[110] This provision enables the Manager and Investment Manager to allow their employees to participate directly without the necessity of creating a new investment vehicle.

[111] As noted earlier, the value is the value of an interest in the Fund as of the close of business on the last business day; that value is used to allow the investment to be deemed to come in as of the first business day of the month.

(b)   The Member Manager may, in its sole discretion, waive any of the foregoing subscription requirements or any sales charge.

(c)   If any Member's Capital Account has a negative balance as a result of the deemed Distributions made to such Member pursuant to Section 8.4,[112] such Member shall contribute to the capital of the Company cash in an amount equal to such negative balance within ten (10) days after notice from the Member Manager of such negative balance.

6.4   Determination of Capital. Capital Account balances and the value of any capital contributed to the Company shall be determined by application of the capital accounting rules in Treas. Reg. § 1.704-1(b)(2)(iv).

6.5   Form of Contribution. Capital contributed by any Member to the Company shall be in the form of cash; except that, in the sole discretion of the Member Manager, any Capital Contribution by any Member may be in the form of Securities. All Securities contributed to the Company shall be valued at their Fair Value.[113]

6.6   No Additional Contributions. After the Closing Date, no Member shall at any time be required, and no Member shall have any right, to make any additional contributions to the Company, except as may be required by law or as set forth in Sections 6.2 and 6.3.[114]

---

[112] This provision deals with withholding taxes paid by the Fund on behalf of (i.e., as the agent for) the investor. Such expenditures are viewed as advances; if the advance exceeds the Member's Capital Account, the Member must repay the advance. This is not a deficit make-up provision. The latter apply on liquidation or termination of an investor's investment.

[113] The contribution of securities could result in a gain recognition even for the contributor. The contributor should consult with his or her tax counsel.

[114] Members do not have preemptive rights and cannot take all of the Fund's capacity without the Manager consenting.

6.7   Use of Capital. The aggregate of all such contributions, net of expenses, shall be available to the Company to carry out the objectives, purposes and powers of the Company.[115]

6.8   No Right to Specific Property. No Member shall have the right to demand to receive specific property, or priority over any other Member, except as is specifically provided herein.

6.9   No Return of Capital Contributions or Interest. No Member is entitled to a return of its Capital Contribution or interest on its Capital Contribution or its Capital Account, except as is specifically provided herein. Each Member shall look solely to Distributions from the Company as provided for herein.

6.10   Grace Period for Contributions. Notwithstanding anything to the contrary contained herein, the Member Manager may, in its sole discretion, permit contributions to the capital of the Company by new or existing Members to be paid into the Company up to ten (10) days following the date on which the Member is to be admitted to the Company in the case of new Members, or on the date the Member's Percentage Interest in the Company is to be increased in the case of existing Members, provided that the Member Manager has received written notice of such new or existing Member's intent to make such contribution by the date of such admission or increase and the Percentage Interest attributable to such contribution shall be set in relation to the value of the Company on the date of final funds availability.[116]

6.11   Advances. If any Member shall advance funds to the Company (an *Advance*), other than as provided in Sections 6.1, 6.2 or 6.3 the amount of

---

[115] This provision means what it says...once the money has been contributed, and even if it is allocated to an Allocation Layer for accounting purposes, it is available to the Fund and is not held in some form of escrow account.

[116] This is a look-back provision that enables the Manager to accept investments that are in transit. Note that the Percentage Interest is NOT determined until the funds are available. This is not a case of backdating—all values will be set as of the availability date.

such Advance shall not be deemed a Capital Contribution, unless the Member Manager expressly agrees otherwise in writing. The amount of such Advance shall be a debt due from the Company to such Member for all purposes, and, except as otherwise expressly agreed at the time such funds are advanced, shall be repaid to such Member as soon as practicable. The lending Member shall have all rights of a creditor against the Company for all purposes. The Member Manager may cause the Company to repay any Advances to the Company in accordance with their terms out of available funds as a priority to any Distributions to the Members under any other provision hereof. Any Advance made by a Member shall bear interest on the unpaid balance at the average cost to the Company of borrowing money, as determined by the Member Manager.[117]

ARTICLE 7
ALLOCATIONS OF GAINS AND LOSSES; DISTRIBUTIONS

7.1   Members' Accounts.

   (a) There will be established on the books of the Company a Capital Account for each Member in accordance with the definitions and methods of allocation prescribed in this Agreement. Each additional Capital Contribution made by a Member to the Company will be designated as a separate Capital Contribution and shall be attributable to a specific Allocation Layer for purposes of determining the Performance Allocations. Allocation Layers will be maintained with respect to any Capital Contribution only so

---

[117] This provision gives the Manager the authority to repay an "advance." This situation can arise where a Manager is "hot" and investors are "throwing money at the Manager" in the hopes that the Manager will take it for the Fund. Despite the doldrums of 2008–2009, believe it or not, this did happen. The provision eliminates most equitable arguments that the Manager should have to invest the money of which he or she has custody.

long as necessary to compute the Performance Allocation attributable to such Allocation Layer.[118]

(b)   The Capital Account of each Member shall be in an amount equal to the sum of such Member's initial Capital Contribution, as adjusted under this Agreement. A Capital Account may be comprised of one or more Allocation Layers (i.e., memoranda capital accounts) as the Member Manager may determine.

(c)   The Capital Accounts will be adjusted and maintained at all times strictly in accordance with Section 704 of the Code and Treas. Reg. §1.704-1(b)(2)(iv) (including, without limitation, Treas. Reg. §§1.704-1(b)(2)(iv)(*d*), 1.704-1(b)(2)(iv)(*f*) and 1.704-1.704-1(b)(2)(iv)(*g*)). The Member Manager is expressly authorized to make appropriate amendments to the allocations of items pursuant to this Article 7 if necessary in order to comply with Section 704 of the Code or Treas. Reg. §1.704-1(b)(2)(iv).

(d)   The Capital Account shall be properly adjusted from time to time, but not less often than the end of each Fiscal Period. Each Member's Capital Account shall be increased by (i) the amount of any cash or the Fair Value of any property contributed (or deemed contributed) by such Member to the Company (net of any liabilities that the Company is considered to assume or take subject to) and (ii) the amount, if any, of Net

---

[118] If the NAV of the Fund increases beyond the highest high water mark of every investor, then all of the Allocation Layers should be able to be rolled up. They no longer have independent significance.

Profits allocated to such Member's Capital Account.[119]

(e) Each Member's Capital Account shall be reduced by (i) the amount, if any, of all Distributions (or deemed Distributions, including deemed Distributions made pursuant to Section 8.4) made to such Member (net of any liabilities that such Member is considered to assume or take subject to), (ii) the amount, if any, of all Net Losses allocated to such Member's Capital Account, (iii) the amount, if any, of all Management Fees allocated to such Member's Capital Account, and (iv) the amount, if any, of all Performance Allocations allocated to such Member's Capital Account.[120]

(f) The Member Manager may create such sub-accounts or memorandum accounts (for either tax and/or book purposes) as it deems necessary or appropriate in its sole discretion in order to properly effect the allocations contemplated by this Agreement.

7.2 Allocation of Net Profits and Net Losses; Performance Allocation.

(a) Except as otherwise provided herein, Net Profits and Net Losses during any Performance Year (or, if necessary, any Fiscal Period[121]) shall be allocated

---

[119] *See* the definition of Net Profit, above. Note that increases in the fair value of an Allocation Layer are included.

[120] *See* the definition of Net Loss above. Note that decreases in the fair value of an Allocation Layer are included.

[121] This parenthetical covers short years of the Fund or of an investment of an investor.

to the Capital Accounts of the Members as of the close of business on the last Business Day of each Performance Year (or, if necessary, each Fiscal Period) in proportion to their respective Capital Account balances as of the end of the last Business Day of such Performance Year or Fiscal Period (after adjusting such Member's Capital Account for any Capital Contributions but not for any withdrawals or Distributions that are effective as of such date) (except that the Member Manager may allocate items of deduction or expense which are paid or incurred by a Member to such Member) (the amount of Net Profits allocated to a particular Member is hereinafter referred to as the *Preliminary Amount*). [122] Net Profits and Net Losses allocated to a Member's Capital Account hereunder shall be further allocated among such Member's Allocation Layers in such manner as the Member Manager deems necessary or appropriate in its sole discretion.

(i)   In the case of the Member Manager, the entire Preliminary Amount initially allocated to its Capital Account shall be finally allocated to that account at the time of such allocation.

(ii)   In the case of a Member, the aggregate of the Preliminary Amounts allocated to the Capital Account of a particular Member for each Fiscal Period in a Performance Year shall be reduced by the Performance Allocation(s), if any, calculated pursuant to Section 7.2(a)(iii), and the remaining

---

[122] The computation is a multi-step process. The purpose of the preliminary amount is to deal with the Manager's investment in the Fund first.

portion of the Preliminary Amount shall be finally allocated to such Member's Capital Account at the end of such Performance Year (or at the time of a Member's withdrawal if such Member's Withdrawal Day is a date other than the last day of a Performance Year).

(iii)   Net Profits shall be allocated to the Member Manager in the amount of the aggregate of the Performance Allocations calculated pursuant to this Section 7.2.

(b)   The Net Losses allocated pursuant to Section 7.2(a) shall not exceed the maximum amount of Net Losses that can be so allocated without causing any Member to have an Adjusted Capital Account Deficit at the end of any Performance Year. In the event some but not all of the Members would have Adjusted Capital Account Deficits as a consequence of an allocation of Losses pursuant to Section 7.2(a) hereof, the limitation set forth in this Section 7.2(b) shall be applied on a Member by Member basis so as to allocate the maximum permissible Net Losses to each Member under §1.704-1(b)(2)(ii)(*d*) of the Treasury Regulations.[123]

(c)   The Member Manager and/or its designee, which may include the Investment Manager will also be entitled to receive, for each Performance Year, a performance allocation (the *Performance Allocation*) in an amount equal to 20 percent of the Net Profit

---

[123] Losses are allocated pro rata—it is only when a Member's Capital Account has been reduced to zero that further allocations of Net Losses stop to that Member until all other Members' Capital Accounts have been reduced to zero.

of the Company allocable to each Allocation Layer other than the Allocation Layers of the Member Manager calculated at the end of each Performance Year (or on the Withdrawal Day of an Allocation Layer, the occurrence of a Liquidating Event or the date of Termination, in each case, if such date is other than the end of a Performance Year) in excess of the High Water Mark (see below) for such Allocation Layer for such Performance Year before giving effect to the Performance Allocation; provided that the Net Profits upon which the Performance Allocation is determined pursuant to this Section 7.2(c) shall not include any Net Profits upon which a Performance Allocation is previously determined and paid pursuant to Section 4.4(a); provided further that, for purposes of calculating Performance Allocations under this Section 7.2(c) and for the avoidance of doubt, Net Profit of the Company allocable to each Allocation Layer will be reduced by the Management Fee allocated under Section 5.4 to each Member who is subject to a Management Fee but shall be computed before the application of the Performance Allocation.[124] Each Capital Contribution made by a Member to the Company will be assigned to a separate Allocation Layer to enable a separate High Water Mark to be maintained for each

---

[124] This clarification is an attempt to prevent an interrelated simultaneous equation for computation of a management fee. The assets of the firm are determined, the capital accounts are grossed up or down to fair value, and then a management fee rate is applied to the Capital Accounts. This happens before the Performance Allocation is computed but after all other expenses, other than the Management Fee, have been taken into account. Similarly, the Performance Allocation is determined after all expenses, including the Management Fee, have been taken into account.

Capital Contribution so long as is necessary properly to compute the Performance Allocation.

(i)   The Performance Allocation is subject to what is commonly referred to as a "High Water Mark" pursuant to which a Performance Allocation is only paid on the new net appreciation in NAV (as calculated before reduction for any Performance Allocation for the current Fiscal Period). The High Water Mark shall be calculated annually. The mechanism used to account for this is an Unrecovered Loss account calculated on an Allocation Layer basis.

(ii)   Once payable, a Performance Allocation will not be reduced by losses incurred in later periods, or repaid by the Company, the Member Manager or the Investment Manager under any circumstances; it is not subject to repayment (i.e. clawback) under any circumstances.[125] Membership Interests that are either purchased or withdrawn during a Performance Year shall be subject to the payment of a Performance Allocation based on the Company's performance during the portion of the Performance Year during which such Membership Interests

---

[125] The high water mark protects investors—if the NAV of an Allocation Layer goes down in value, then the Manager receives no Performance Allocation with respect to that Layer until the NAV of that Layer recovers. To also allow the Investor a clawback, it distorts the shared gain proposition. Congress has suggested that the Performance Allocation is in effect a fee and should be taxed as ordinary income. If that is the case, few people would be willing to return a fee earned. A clawback provision means that the Manager never really knows what his or her income is until the Fund liquidates, because in the face of a clawback provision, he or she holds the Performance Allocation only under a claim of right.

were held by the Member. Appropriate adjustments may be made by the Member Manager in its discretion to account for subscriptions and withdrawals.

(iii)   The Performance Allocation is not prorated for the actual time that an investor held a Membership Interest during a Performance Year.[126]

(iv)   If a Member withdraws at a time when the Member has an Unrecovered Loss because the Allocation Layer withdrawn is below its High Water Mark, then the Member's entire Unrecovered Loss for that Allocation Layer shall be reduced in proportion to the portion of the Capital Account withdrawn over the total Capital Account of the Member.

(v)   If more than one entity has served as Member Manager during a particular Performance Year, the Performance Allocation for such Performance Year shall be allocated between or among the entities that served as Member Manager during such Performance Year based on a proportion computed on the number of

---

[126] Performance Allocations are never adjusted based on time—it is quite possible that the NAV increase can occur in a very short period of time while the rest of the year was flat. An investment on October 1 can increase in value during the last few months of the year as an investment made on January 1 of that same year. The Performance Allocation is based on the delta between the beginning and ending values.

days as Manager over the total number of days during the year. The sharing is further weighted based on the relative size of the Company during the year of transition.[127].

(vi)   To the extent that a Performance Allocation is made at the Company level, the Company will not be charged an incentive fee or performance allocation at the Master Fund level. [128]

(vii)   The Member Manager may elect to waive all or any part of the Performance Allocation with respect to any Member at its sole discretion and without consent of or notice to any Member. Further, the Member Manager may cause all or a portion of its Performance Allocation to

---

[127] Because positive and/or negative performance can occur over a very brief time during a calendar year (i.e., the market can run up all on the last day, after having been flat for the entire year), it is not appropriate for a year during which the manager will be changing to treat each period of time that a different Manager provided services as a separate year for purposes of computing the Performance Allocation. That could result in an allocation being made to the first manager during the year (or the second) but none for the rest. Investors would be peeved (and rightfully so) if they paid a performance allocation to the first manager but by the end of the year performance was negative and no Performance Allocation would have been due at the end of the year. Because the Model Agreement does not have a clawback, another mechanism is needed. For the year of transition, the Performance Allocation for the entire year is computed. It is then allocated on a days-managed-over-total-days-in-the-year basis. The computation is further weighted based on the relative size of the Fund for each period.

[128] As a practical matter, there is no effective way to compute a Performance Allocation at the Master Fund level. Each investor should have a separate Allocation Layer value. While it could be done by having separate Allocation Layers at the Master Fund level and then flowing them through to the Feeder on an investor-by-investor basis, the promoter and Member Manager may unwittingly cause the Feeder to lose its tax efficacy using this strategy.

be paid to another party, including one of its Affiliates and any sub-adviser, at its sole discretion and without consent of or notice to any Members.

(viii)   The "*Unrecovered Losses*" with respect to an Allocation Layer of a Member at any given time shall be the sum of all prior Net Losses allocated to such Allocation Layer that have not been subsequently offset by Net Profits; provided, however, that the Unrecovered Losses shall be reduced proportionately to reflect any withdrawals made by such Member, and other applicable adjustments.

(ix)   In the event that the Company is dissolved other than as of the end of a Performance Year (or a Member is permitted or required to withdraw from the Company other than as of the end of a Performance Year), the applicable Performance Allocation shall be determined for the period from the commencement of the Company's Performance Year through the occurrence of a Liquidating Event (or, with respect to a withdrawing Member, the applicable Withdrawal Day) and allocated to the account of the Member Manager and/or to the account of any investment manager, sub-adviser and/or private placement agent (with which an investment manager may be sharing the Performance Allocations) that the Member Manager, on behalf of the Company, has designated to share the Performance Allocation with the Member Manager. Following the occurrence of a Liquidating Event, the applicable Performance Allocation shall be determined for the period from the day after the occurrence of the Liquidating Event through the earlier of the end of the Performance Year or Termination. Thereafter, the applicable Performance Allocation shall be determined for the period from the commencement of the Performance Year through the earlier of the end of the Performance Year or Termination.

(x) With respect to an Allocation Layer, if in any Performance Year the Company does not generate a Preliminary Amount sufficient to restore any Unrecovered Loss for an Allocation Layer, the Member Manager will not be entitled to any Performance Allocation with respect to that Allocation Layer for that Performance Year or thereafter for as long as such Unrecovered Loss remains.[129]

(xi) The Performance Allocations so determined pursuant to this Section 7.2(c) and pursuant to Section 4.4(a) shall constitute reallocations of Net Profits [130]as of the end of the Performance Year to which they relate (or, if necessary, items of gross income, in which event Net Profits

---

[129] This is the provision that operationalizes the High Water Mark.

[130] This is the provision that preserves the character of the Performance Allocation for the Manager/Investment Manager. This may be a moot point; however, if the investment style of the Fund results in the Fund not holding assets for a sufficient time to meet the long-term holding period (i.e., more than one year) for capital gain status. Also, Congress has taken aim at these provisions in recent legislative proposals.

and, if necessary Net Losses will be redetermined and allocated in order to effectuate the allocation of the Performance Allocations) away from the Members with respect to whose Capital Accounts such amounts relate and to the Member Manager; and the amount of Net Profits or Net Losses finally allocated to each Member during each Performance Year (or Fiscal Period) to which such reallocation relates shall be determined after giving effect to the reallocations hereunder.

(xii)   The intent of Sections 7.2(c) and 4.4(a) is to allocate to the Member Manager (in its capacity as a Member) a Performance Allocation with respect to the increase in the Net Asset Value of the Company attributable to the increase in value of amounts invested or continued in the Company by each Member during each Performance Year (or other relevant period).

(xiii)   The Performance Allocation shall not result in the creation of or the increase in the amount of Unrecovered Losses in the Allocation Layer with respect to which the Performance Allocation relates. This Agreement shall be interpreted in a manner consistent with the foregoing intent and the intent of this Section 7.2(c).

(xiv)   At the end of each Performance Year, the Capital Accounts will be finally adjusted by taking into account all contributions, Distributions, Management Fees, allocations of Net Profits and Net Losses, Performance Allocations and other adjustments. The application and determination of the Performance Allocations, including, without limitation, all allocations of Net Profits and Net Losses, and all other issues and interpretations incident or related thereto, shall be made by the Member Manager, whose determinations with respect thereto shall be final.

(d) If any Member shall withdraw from the Company under any provision of this Agreement as of the end of a Fiscal Period, and if such Member's Capital Account as of the end of that Fiscal Period (after taking into account any allocations and other adjustments under this Agreement, other than the withdrawal itself, through the end of such Fiscal Period) differs from his adjusted income tax basis in his interest in the Company (for the purpose of this Section 7.2(d), tax basis shall be determined by disregarding any liabilities that would otherwise be included in such income tax basis), then, notwithstanding anything to the contrary herein, for income tax purposes, the Member Manager shall have the sole discretion to make a supplemental allocation of the Company's items of taxable income and gain (if such Capital Account exceeds the tax basis) or loss and deduction (if the tax basis exceeds such Capital Account) for such Fiscal Period to the withdrawing Member in an amount not to exceed the amount necessary to equalize such income tax basis immediately after such allocation but before the withdrawal.[131] In the event that more than one

---

[131] Given the unique nature of a Fund as a partnership for federal tax purposes, withdrawals give the Fund an opportunity to shift taxable gain to the withdrawing member.

Member having such a discrepancy between his Capital Account and the tax basis of his Membership Interest shall withdraw at the end of the same Fiscal Period, any allocations pursuant to this Section 7.2(d) shall be in proportion to the relative size of the discrepancies.

(e)   The following is intended to serve as a theoretical and simplified example regarding Performance Allocation calculation for the Company and is meant as an illustration and not a limitation or otherwise and does not limit the otherwise applicable discretion of the Member Manager under this Agreement in any fashion. The example below does not illustrate the deduction for the Management Fee, which is deducted from Net Profits prior to determining the amount of the Performance Allocation and for the sake of simplicity, uses proportional allocations as an exercise of the Member Manager's discretion which may not be the allocation method chosen by the Member Manager.[132]

Day 1: Assume that the Company has two Members A and B, each of whom invested $1 million at inception of the Company. On Day 1, the current valuation of the net assets of the Company (the *NAV*) is $2 million.

Day 365: Assume at the end of the first Performance Year the NAV of the Company has dropped to $1.5 million. The Net Loss of $500,000, the difference between the beginning

---

[132] This example speaks for itself. It allows for a clear reflection of the Performance Allocation among the Members and their Allocation Layers in both up and down markets.

NAV of $2 million and the ending NAV of $1.5 million, is allocated $250,000 to each of A and B, resulting in ending Capital Accounts of $750,000 each. A and B each have an Unrecovered Loss of $250,000 with respect to their Allocation Layer. Another way to describe this is that each of A and B has a High Water Mark of $1 million.

Day 1 of Year 2: Investor A invests an additional $1 million, increasing A's Capital Account to $1.75 million. The additional investment creates a second Allocation Layer. A's Percentage Interest as of the commencement of Year 2 is 70 percent ($1.75 million Capital Account over $2.5 million sum of all Capital Accounts). A's Allocation Layer Percentage in the first Allocation Layer is 42.86 percent ($750,000/$1.75 million) and in the second Allocation Layer is 57.14 percent ($1 million/$1.75 million). B's Percentage Interest as of the commencement of Year 2 is 30 percent ($750,000 Capital Account over $2.5 million sum of all Capital Accounts).

Day 365 of Year 2: Assume that the NAV of the Company is $3 million. Because no new investors are admitted as Members and no new investments are made during Year 2, the ending Percentage Interests of the Members are the same as their beginning Percentage Interests. Net Profit is $500,000, the difference between the ending NAV of $3 million and the beginning NAV of $2.5 million.

The Preliminary Amount allocated to B's Capital Account is $150,000 (30 percent of the $500,000 Net Profit). No Performance Allocation applies to B's Capital Account because Net Profits allocated to B are less than B's Unrecovered

Loss. Accordingly, the entire Preliminary Amount of $150,000 of Net Profits is allocated to B.

B's ending Capital Account is $900,000 ($750,000 plus $150,000) and B has an Unrecovered Loss of $100,000 (Unrecovered Loss from Year 1 of $250,000 reduced by $150,000 allocation of Net Profits in Year 2).

The Preliminary Amount allocated to A's Capital Account is $350,000 (70 percent of the $500,000 Net Profit). The $350,000 Preliminary Amount is allocated to A's Allocation Layers as follows: $150,000 to A's first Allocation Layer ($350,000 times $750,000/$1.75 million) and $200,000 to A's second Allocation Layer ($350,000 times $1 million/$1.75 million).

A has an Unrecovered Loss of $250,000 in his first Allocation Layer. The $150,000 of Net Profits from Year 2 reduces the Unrecovered Loss to $100,000 ($250,000 - $150,000) (the same as B). There is no Performance Allocation with respect to A's first Allocation Layer because the amount of Net Profits allocated to the first Allocation Layer is less than the existing Unrecovered Loss. Therefore, $150,000 is finally allocated to A's first Allocation Layer and A's Unrecovered Loss for that Layer is $100,000.

A has no Unrecovered Loss in the second Allocation Layer, because A's second Allocation Layer has not previously been allocated Net Losses. The Performance Allocation attributable to A's second Allocation Layer is $40,000 (20 percent of $200,000 Net Profits allocated to the second Allocation Layer). Therefore, $160,000 of the Preliminary Amount is finally allocated to A's second Allocation Layer and $40,000 is allocated to the Capital Account of the Member Manager.

A's ending Capital Account is $2.06 million ($1.75 million beginning Capital Account plus $310,000 Net Profits). The Capital Account attributable to the first Allocation Layer is $900,000 ($750,000 plus $150,000 allocated to the first Allocation Layer) and the Capital Account attributable to the second Allocation Layer is $1.16 million ($1 million plus $160,000 allocated to the second Allocation Layer). The Allocation Layer Percentage for the first Layer is 43.69 percent ($900,000/$2.06 million) and for the second Layer is ($1.16 million/$2.06 million) 56.31percent.

The Percentage Interests of the Members at the beginning of Year 3 are as follows: A's Percentage Interest is 68.67 percent ($2.06 million/ $3 ,illion), B's Percentage Interest is 30 percent ($900,000/$3 million) and the Member Manager's Percentage Interest is 1.33 percent($40,000/$3 million).

Day 365 of Year 3: Assume the NAV of the Company is $3.5 million. Net Profit is $500,000 ($3.5 million ending NAV less $3,000,000 beginning NAV). No new Members are admitted and no Member makes an additional Capital Contribution. For these computation purposes, Capital Account balances are computed without regard to profit identified during the Year.

The Preliminary Amount allocated to B is (($900,000/$3 million) * $500,000) and B's ending Capital Account is $1.05 million. The allocation of Net Profits to B reduces B's existing Unrecovered Loss of $100,000 to zero. The

$50,000 of Net Profits in excess of B's Unrecovered Loss is subject to a Performance Allocation of $10,000 (20 percent of $50,000). Thus, $140,000 is finally allocated to B's Capital Account and $10,000 is allocated to the Capital Account of the Member Manager.

The Preliminary Amount allocated to A is $343,333.33 ($2.060 million $3 million * $500,000). Of this amount, $150,000 is allocated to the first Allocation Layer ($900,000/$2.06 million * $343,333.33). The allocation of Net Profits to A's first Allocation Layer reduces A's existing Unrecovered Loss of $100,000 to zero. The $50,000 of Net Profits in excess of A's Unrecovered Loss is subject to a Performance Allocation of $10,000 (20 percnet of $50,000). Thus, $140,000 is finally allocated to A's first Allocation Layer and $10,000 is allocated to the Capital Account of the Member Manager.

The Preliminary Amount allocated to A's second Allocation Layer is $193,333.33 (($1.16 million/$2.06 million) * $343,333.33). Because A has no Unrecovered Loss with respect to the second Allocation Layer, the Net Profits are subject to a Performance Allocation on this Allocation Layer equal to $38,666.66 (20 percent of $193,333.33). Therefore, $154,666.67 is finally allocated to A's second Allocation Layer and $38,666.66 is allocated to the Member Manager. Because A has no remaining Unrecovered Losses, it will no longer be necessary to maintain the two separate Allocation Layers and the amounts in the first and second Allocation Layers will be combined. If A makes an additional Capital Contribution, a new Allocation Layer will be created.

The Member Manager is allocated Net Profits of ($40,000/3 million) * 500,000 = $6,666.66. The Member Manager's Net Profits are not subject to a Performance Allocation.

Total Performance Allocations for Year 3 are $58,666.66.

A's Capital Account is $2,354,666.67 ($2.06 million plus $140,000 plus $154,666.67).

B's Capital Account is $1.04 million ($900,000 plus $140,000).

The Member Manager's Capital Account is $105,333.33 ($40,000 plus $6,666.66 plus $58,666.67).

7.3   Tax Allocations.

(a)   In accordance with Code §704(c) and the Treasury Regulations there under, income, gain, loss, and deduction with respect to any property contributed to the capital of the Company shall, solely for tax purposes, be allocated among the Members so as to take account of any variation between the adjusted basis of such property to the Company for federal income tax purposes and its initial Fair Value.

(b)   Except as otherwise provided herein, all items of taxable income, gain, loss, deduction, and any other allocations not otherwise provided for shall be allocated among the Members in the same proportion as such Member's share of Net Profits or Net Losses, as the case may be, for the Performance Year (or Fiscal Period or other allocation period); provided, however, that the Member Manager may, in its sole discretion, first allocate items of taxable income, gain, loss and deduction to a Withdrawing Member in such a manner that, to the extent possible, any unrealized appreciation or depreciation in the Company interest withdrawn is eliminated.

(c)   Any elections or other decisions relating to such allocations shall be made by the Member Manager in any manner that reasonably reflects the purpose and intention of this Agreement. Allocations pursuant to this Section 7.3 are solely for purposes of federal, state, and local taxes and shall not affect, or in any way be taken into account in computing, any Member's Capital Account or share of Net Profits, Net Losses, other items, or Distributions pursuant to any provision of this Agreement.

7.4   Special Allocations. The following special allocations shall be made in the following order:

(a)   Minimum Gain Chargeback. Except as otherwise provided in §1.704-2(f) of the Treasury Regulations, notwithstanding any other provision of this Article 7, if there is a net decrease in Partnership Minimum Gain during any Performance Year, each Member shall be specially allocated items of Company income and gain for such Performance Year (and, if necessary, subsequent Performance Years) in an amount equal to such Member's share of the net decrease in Partnership Minimum Gain, determined in accordance with Treasury Regulations §1.704-2(g). Allocations pursuant to the previous sentence shall be made in proportion to the respective amounts required to be allocated to each Member pursuant thereto. The items to be so allocated shall be determined in accordance with §§1.704-2(f)(6) and 1.704-2(j)(2) of the Treasury

Regulations. This Section 7.4(a) is intended to comply with the minimum gain chargeback requirement in §1.704-2(f) of the Treasury Regulations and shall be interpreted consistently therewith.

(b) <u>Partner Minimum Gain Chargeback</u>. Except as otherwise provided in §1.704-2(i)(4) of the Treasury Regulations, notwithstanding any other provision of this Article 7, if there is a net decrease in Partner Nonrecourse Debt Minimum Gain attributable to a Partner Nonrecourse Debt during any Performance Year, each Member who has a share of the Partner Nonrecourse Debt Minimum Gain attributable to such Partner Nonrecourse Debt, determined in accordance with §1.704-2(i)(5) of the Treasury Regulations, shall be specially allocated items of Company income and gain for such Performance Year (and, if necessary, subsequent Performance Years) in an amount equal to such Member's share of the net decrease in Partner Nonrecourse Debt Minimum Gain attributable to such Partner Nonrecourse Debt, determined in accordance with Treasury Regulations §1.704-2(i)(4). Allocations pursuant to the previous sentence shall be made in proportion to the respective amounts required to be allocated to each Member pursuant thereto. The items to be so allocated shall be determined in accordance with §§1.704-2(i)(4) and 1.704-2(j)(2) of the Treasury Regulations. This Section 7.4(b) is intended to comply with the minimum gain chargeback requirement in §1.704-2(i)(4) of the Treasury Regulations and shall be interpreted consistently therewith.

(c) <u>Qualified Income Offset</u>. In the event any Member unexpectedly receives any adjustments, allocations, or Distributions described in §1.704-1(b)(2)(ii)(d)(4), §1.704-1(b)(2)(ii)(d)(5) or §1.704-1(b)(2)(ii)(d)(6) of the Treasury Regulations, items of Company income and gain shall be specially allocated to each such Member in an amount and manner sufficient to eliminate, to the extent required by the Treasury Regulations, the Adjusted Capital Account Deficit of such Member as quickly as possible, provided that an allocation pursuant to this Section 7.4(c) shall be made only if and to the extent that such Member would have an Adjusted Capital Account Deficit after all other allocations provided for in this Article 7 have been tentatively made as if this Section 7.4(c) were not in the Agreement. [133]

(d)   <u>Gross Income Allocation.</u> In the event any Member has a deficit Capital Account at the end of any Company Performance Year which is in excess of the sum of (i) the amount such Member is obligated to restore pursuant to any provision of this Agreement, and (ii) the amount such Member is deemed to be obligated to restore pursuant to the penultimate sentences of Treasury Regulations §§1.704-2(g)(1) and 1.704-2(i)(5), each such Member shall be specially allocated items of Company income and gain in the amount of such excess as quickly as possible, provided that an allocation pursuant to this Section 7.4(d) shall be

---

[133] Because the Fund does not have a deficit make-up provision, a Qualified Income Offset (QIO) is necessary to make the allocations have substantial economic effect for federal tax purposes. In contrast, many private equity funds merely have tax follow cash—as cash is distributed, the tax incidents follow the distributions. Such mechanisms do not work in hedge funds, because most hedge funds reinvest proceeds from investment operations and rarely make distributions. Thus, hedge funds and funds of funds are required to stay within the Section 704 rules, and that included a QIO.

made only if and to the extent that such Member would have a deficit Capital Account in excess of such sum after all other allocations provided for in this Article 7 have been made as if Section 7.4(c) hereof and this Section 7.4(d) were not in the Agreement.

(e)   Nonrecourse   Deductions.   Nonrecourse Deductions for any Performance Year shall be allocated in accordance with each Member's Percentage Interest.

(f)   Partner Nonrecourse Deductions. Any Partner Nonrecourse Deductions for any Performance Year shall be specially allocated to the Member who bears the economic risk of loss with respect to the Partner Nonrecourse Debt to which such Partner Nonrecourse Deductions are attributable in accordance with Treasury Regulations §1.704-2(i)(1).

(g)   Section 754 Adjustments. To the extent an adjustment to the adjusted tax basis of any Company asset pursuant to Code §734(b) or Code §743(b) is required, pursuant to Treasury Regulations §1.704-1(b)(2)(iv)(m), to be taken into account in determining Capital Accounts the amount of such adjustment to Capital Accounts shall be treated as an item of gain (if the adjustment increases the basis of the asset) or loss (if the adjustment decreases such basis) and such gain or loss shall be specially allocated to the Members in a manner consistent with the manner in which their Capital Accounts are required to be adjusted pursuant to such Regulation.[134]

(h)   <u>Imputed Interest</u>[135]. If the Company has taxable interest income with respect to any promissory note pursuant to Section 483 of the Code or Sections 1271 through 1288 of the Code:

    (i)   Such interest income shall be specially allocated to the Member to whom such promissory note relates; and

    (ii)   The amount of such interest income shall be excluded from the Capital Contribution credited to such Member's Capital Account in connection with payments of principal on such promissory note.

(i)   Syndication Expenses.

    (i)   Syndication Expenses for any Performance Year or other period shall be allocated to the Members in proportion to their Percentage Interests; provided that if additional Members are admitted to the Company on different dates, all Syndication Expenses shall be divided among those who are Members from time to time so that, to the extent possible, the cumulative

---

[134] As noted above in footnote 15, Funds rarely make 754 elections because of the mischief that a transfer of a partnership interest could cause to the Fund's tax basis in its assets. Nevertheless, the Model Agreement includes that authority and also includes the tax provisions for dealing with the consequences of the election.

[135] This refers to imputed interest where the Fund and a member are parties to the promissory note that is giving rise to the imputed interest. This does not refer to notes purchased as investments by the Fund or the Master Fund.

Syndication Expenses are allocated in proportion to the Percentage Interests from time to time. If the Member Manager determines that such result is not likely to be achieved through future allocations of Syndication Expenses, the Member Manager may allocate a portion of Net Profits or Net Losses to achieve the same effect on the Capital Accounts of the Members, notwithstanding any other provision of this Agreement.[136]

(ii) Notwithstanding the foregoing, if a particular Member or Members agree to pay some or all of the Syndication Expenses for any Performance Year or other period, such Syndication Expenses shall be allocated to such Member.

7.5   Curative Allocations. The allocations set forth in Sections 7.4(a), 7.4(b), 7.4(c), 7.4(d), 7.4(e), 7.4(f), and 7.4(g) hereof (the *Regulatory Allocations*) are intended to comply with certain requirements of the Treasury Regulations. It is the intent of the Members that, to the extent possible, all Regulatory Allocations shall be offset either with other Regulatory Allocations or with special allocations of other items of Company income, gain, loss, or deduction pursuant to this Section 7.5. Therefore, notwithstanding any other provision of this Article 7 (other than the Regulatory Allocations), the Manager may, in its discretion, make such offsetting special allocations of Company income, gain, loss or deduction in whatever manner it determines appropriate so that, after such offsetting allocations are made, each Member's Capital Account balance is, to the extent possible, equal to the Capital Account balance such Member would

---

[136] Because syndication expenses are neither deductible nor amortizable, the Model Agreement allocates them to investors; it also allows investors to pay for their share, thus allowing the Fund to reflect a return that is not affected by these expenditures.

have had if the Regulatory Allocations were not part of the Agreement and all Company items were allocated pursuant to Section 7.3 (other than Section 7.2(a)(i)). In exercising its discretion under this Section 7.5, the Manager may take into account future Regulatory Allocations under Sections 7.4(a) and 7.4(b) that, although not yet made, are likely to offset other Regulatory Allocations previously made under Sections 7.4(e) and 7.4(f).

7.6   Other Allocation Rules.

>   (a)   For purposes of determining the Net Profits, Net Losses, or any other items allocable to any period, Net Profits, Net Losses, and any such other items shall be determined by the Member Manager using any permissible method under Code §706 and the Treasury Regulations thereunder.[137]

>   (b)   The Members are aware of the income tax consequences of the allocations made by this Article 7 and hereby agree to be bound by the provisions of this Article 7 in reporting their shares of Company income and loss for income tax purposes.

>   (c)   Notwithstanding any of the foregoing provisions to the contrary, if taxable gain to be allocated includes income resulting from the sale or disposition of Company property or property of a limited partnership or joint venture in which the Company owns an interest that is treated as ordinary income, such gain so treated as ordinary income shall be allocated to and reported by each Member in proportion to allocations to that Member of the items that gave rise to such

---

[137] Agreements need savings clauses such as this to enable to Fund to achieve its intended purposes.

ordinary income, and the Company shall keep records of such allocations. In the event of the subsequent admission of any new Member, any item that would constitute "unrealized receivables" under Section 751 of the Code and the Regulations thereunder shall not be shared by the newly admitted Members, but rather shall be allocated to existing Members.

7.7   Safe Harbor Election and Forfeiture Allocations.[138]

(a)   The Member Manager is hereby authorized, on behalf of all Members, to cause the Company to make an election to value any interest in the Company that may be granted as compensation for services rendered to or on behalf of the Company (the *Compensatory Interest*) at liquidation value (the *Safe Harbor Election*), as the same may be permitted pursuant to or in accordance with the finally promulgated successor rules to Proposed Treasury Regulations Section 1.83-3(l) and IRS Notice 2005-43 (collectively, the *Proposed Rules*). The Member Manager shall cause the Company to make any allocations of items of income, gain, deduction, loss, or credit (including forfeiture allocations and elections as to allocation periods) necessary or appropriate to effectuate and maintain the Safe Harbor Election.

---

[138] Is the grant of a profits-only interest in a partnership immediately taxable (as would be a grant of a share of stock in a corporation), or is it only taxable when profits are actually allocated to the holder? If the former, what is the value that is subject to tax and when? The IRS Notice referenced above settles this issue (in proposed form). A compensatory grant is taxable, but it will be valued at its liquidation value on grant (which should be zero for a profits-only interest). If the grant affected a shift of any of the residual equity value of the business, then that would be outside the safe harbor.

(b)   Any such Safe Harbor Election shall be binding on the Company and on all of its Members with respect to all transfers of the Compensatory Interest thereafter made by the Company while a Safe Harbor Election is in effect. A Safe Harbor Election once made may be revoked by the Member Manager as permitted by the Proposed Rules or any applicable rule.

(c)   Each Member, by signing this Agreement or by accepting such transfer of a Membership Interest, hereby agrees to comply with all requirements of the Safe Harbor Election with respect to the Compensatory Interest while the Safe Harbor Election remains effective, and to file all tax returns consistent with such Safe Harbor Election.

(d)   The Member Manager shall file or cause the Company to file all returns, reports and other documentation as may be required to perfect and maintain the Safe Harbor Election with respect to transfers of all or part of the Compensatory Interest.

(e)   The Member Manager is hereby authorized and empowered, without further consent or action of the Members, to amend the Agreement as necessary to comply with the Proposed Rules or any rule, in order to provide for a Safe Harbor Election and the ability to maintain or revoke the same, and shall have the authority to execute any such amendment by and on behalf of each Member. Any undertakings by the Members necessary to enable or preserve a Safe Harbor Election may be reflected in such amendments and to the extent so reflected shall be binding on each Member, respectively, provided, that such amendments are not reasonably likely to have a material adverse effect on the rights and obligations of the Members.

(f)   Each Member agrees to cooperate with the Member Manager to perfect and maintain any Safe Harbor Election, and to timely execute and deliver any documentation with respect thereto reasonably requested by the Member Manager.

(g)   No transfer, assignment or other disposition of any interest in the Company by a Member shall be effective unless prior to such transfer, assignment or disposition the transferee, assignee or intended recipient of such interest shall have agreed in writing to be bound by the provisions of this Section 7.7 in form satisfactory to the Member Manager.

7.8   Distributions.

(a)   The Member Manager shall be solely responsible for making all determinations, in its sole and absolute discretion, of amounts, timing, and type of all Distributions to Members, if any. [139]

(b)   All Distributions shall be made to the Members pro rata in proportion to their Percentage Interests.

(c)   In the sole discretion of the Member Manager, Securities, assets, investments or other property in-kind may be distributed to the Members. Each in-kind Distribution of Securities, assets, investments or other property shall be distributed

---

[139] The Member Manager's authority is plenary and absolute. Ordinarily, Funds of this sort do not make periodic distributions, opting instead to reinvest all proceeds in new investments.

in accordance with this Section 7.8 as if there had been a sale of such property for an amount of cash equal to the fair value of such property (as determined by the Member Manager) followed by an immediate distribution of such cash proceeds. Distributions consisting of Securities, assets, investments or other property shall be made, to the extent practicable, in pro rata portions as to each Member receiving such Distributions. For purposes of the preceding sentence, Securities, assets, investments, or other property having a different tax basis than like Securities, assets, investments or other property shall be considered to be Securities, assets, investments or other property of a different type.

(d)   In the event of such in-kind Distribution of Securities as described in Section 7.8(c), above, Securities or instruments that do not have a readily ascertainable value will be valued by the Member Manager taking into account such factors as the original purchase price of the Securities or instruments, estimates of liquidation value of such Securities or instruments, the liquidity of such Securities or instruments, projected cash flows of the issuers of such Securities or instruments, and changes in the financial conditions and prospects of such issuers. Amounts distributed to any Member pursuant to this Section 7.8 shall be debited to such Member's Capital Account and, if necessary, appropriate adjustments shall be made to the Net Asset Value of the Company attributable to such Capital Account.

(e)   Any Distributions made pursuant hereto shall be allocated to each Allocation Layer in such a manner as the Manager deems necessary or appropriate in its sole discretion.

7.9   Limitations on Distributions and Withdrawal Payments.

(a)   The Company shall not make a Distribution or withdrawal payment to a Member to the extent that at the time of the Distribution or withdrawal payment, after giving effect to the Distribution or withdrawal payment, all liabilities of the Company (other than liabilities to Members on account of their Membership Interests and liabilities for which the recourse of creditors is limited to specified property of the Company) exceed the fair value of the assets and/or investments of the Company.[140]

(b)   A Member who receives a Distribution or withdrawal payment in violation of Section 7.9(a), and who knew at the time of the Distribution or withdrawal payment that the Distribution or withdrawal payment violated Section 7.9(a), shall be liable to the Company for the amount of the Distribution or withdrawal payment (as applicable), together with interest thereon. A Member who receives a Distribution or withdrawal payment in violation of Section 7.9(a), and who did not know at the time of the Distribution or withdrawal payment that the Distribution or withdrawal payment violated Section 7.9(a), shall not be liable for the amount of the Distribution or withdrawal payment (as applicable).

(c)   No Distribution pursuant to this Agreement shall be made if such Distribution would violate the Act;

---

[140] Indemnification obligations under the Model Agreement will reduce cash/assets available for distribution.

(d)   Except as provided in Section 8.4, no Distribution shall be made to (A) a Member if, after giving effect to such Distribution, such Member's Capital Account shall have a negative balance or (B) the Member Manager in its capacity as a Member if such Distribution would result in a violation of Section 4.6; and

(e)   Except as provided in Section 8.4, no Distribution shall be made if such Distribution would violate the applicable terms of any agreement or any other instrument to which the Company is a party.

(f)   In the event of any postponement of a Distribution to be made pursuant to this Agreement, (i) such capital so retained by the Company shall continue to be subject to all debts and obligations of the Company, and (ii) the Member Manager shall use its best efforts to make such Distribution as soon as may reasonably be practicable; except that the Member Manager need not take any action which it, in its sole discretion, considers to be disadvantageous to the Company as a whole.

7.10   Member Manager Tax Distributions.

(a)   The Member Manager may cause the Company to tentatively distribute to the Member Manager (in its capacity as a Member) during each Performance Year amounts reasonably required by the Member Manager for payment of its federal, state and local estimated (or other) taxes (and/or for payment by its beneficial owners of such taxes) in each case relating to the Member Manager's distributive share of the income of the Company (*Tentative Distributions*), by giving thirty (30) days prior written notice to the Company, which notice shall state the amount of the Tentative Distribution.[141]

(b)   If the aggregate of all Tentative Distributions to the Member Manager during a Performance Year is less than or equal to the Performance Allocations (as set forth in Sections 7.2(c) and Section 4.4(a)) for such Performance Year, the amount of such Tentative Distributions shall be treated as distributed to the Member Manager and debited from the Capital Account of the Member Manager as of the last day of such Performance Year.

(c)   If the aggregate of all Tentative Distributions to the Member Manager during a Performance Year exceeds the Performance Allocations for such Performance Year, an amount of such Tentative Distributions equal to such Performance Allocations shall be treated as distributed to the Member Manager and debited from the Capital Account of the Member Manager as of the last day of such Performance Year, and the excess of such Tentative Distributions over such Performance Allocations shall be treated as a loan from the Company to the Member Manager, bearing interest at the Applicable Federal Rate on the amount of such excess from time to time. For purposes of this Agreement, "*Applicable Federal Rate*" means the rate for short-term demand loans

---

[141] The Model Agreement recognizes that the operation of the Fund is likely to be a significant source of revenue for the Member Manager. If the Member Manager allows its Performance Allocation to stay invested in the Fund, the Member Manager may nevertheless ask the Fund for a distribution to enable the Member Manager to pay its taxes. The Model Agreement contains an adjustment mechanism that recognizes that estimated taxes paid during the year may overstate allocable taxes.

as published by the US Department of the Treasury from time to time as applicable for the days on which any Tentative Distributions are treated as loans under this Section 7.10.

(d)   Any amount treated as a loan from the Company to the Member Manager pursuant to Section 7.10(c) shall be repaid by the Member Manager to the Company as soon as practicable after the close of the Performance Year, taking into consideration the timing of the receipt, if any, of a refund of estimated taxes for such Performance Year and estimated tax payments required to be made in the subsequent Performance Year; provided, that the Member Manager may elect at any time to repay such loan by debiting its Capital Account by the amount of such loan, together with accrued and unpaid interest.

7.11   Interest on and Return of Capital Contributions. No Member shall be entitled to interest on its Capital Contributions or Capital Account balance, or to a return of its Capital Contributions except as otherwise provided in this Agreement.[142]

ARTICLE 8
TAXES

8.1   Elections. The Member Manager shall make any and all elections on behalf of the Company under the Code and any other applicable tax law as the Member Manager shall deem to be in the best interests of the Company. The Member Manager shall prepare or cause to be prepared and shall file on or before the due date (or any extension thereof) any tax returns that shall be required to be filed by the Company. The Member Manager shall cause the Company to pay any taxes payable by the

---

[142] The investor will receive a return based on the Fund's return.

Company; provided, however, that the Member Manager shall not be required to cause the Company to pay any tax so long as the Member Manager or the Company shall in good faith and by appropriate legal proceedings be contesting the validity, applicability, or amount of such tax without materially endangering any rights or interests of the Company.

8.2   Tax Matters Partner. The Member Manager is designated as the Company's "Tax Matters Partner" pursuant to § 6231(a)(7) of the Code, and, to the extent authorized or permitted under applicable law, the Member Manager is authorized and required to represent the Company and each Member in connection with all examinations of the Company's affairs by tax authorities, including resulting administrative and judicial proceedings, and to expend Company funds for professional services and costs connected therewith. Each Member agrees to cooperate with the Member Manager and to do or refrain from doing any and all such things reasonably required by the Member to conduct such proceedings. Each Member must provide a Form W-8 or W-9 (or acceptable substitute) as a condition to the acceptance of such Member's subscription. Each Member must update its Form W-8 or Form W-9 as required by applicable law and deliver such updated Form W-8 or Form W-9 to the Company within ten (10) Business Days of the event that required the Form W-8 or Form W-9 to be updated.

8.3   Tax Liability. If the Company shall be deemed to be an entity separately subject to any tax (whether or not such tax shall be payable or shall have been paid by the Company or the Member Manager, although the Member Manager shall not be obligated to do so), each Member (or transferee, if any) shall be liable for and pay to the Company or the Member Manager, upon the Member Manager's request, an amount that shall be determined pro rata in accordance with the respective Capital Accounts of the Members at the close of business (as determined by the Member Manager in its sole discretion) on the last day of the period for which such tax shall have been assessed. Alternatively, if the Company and/or the Member Manager shall have paid any such tax out of its own funds (although the Member Manager shall not be obligated to do so), upon a distribution of funds to a Member (or transferee) or a withdrawal by a Member (or transferee) of all or a portion of its Capital Account, all amounts of such taxes may be deducted from the proceeds of such distribution or withdrawal and reimbursed to the Company and/or the Member Manager.

8.4   Withholding Tax. If the Company is required to withhold United States taxes on income with respect to interests held by Members which are nonresident alien individuals, foreign corporations, foreign partnerships, foreign trusts, or foreign estates, the Member Manager shall withhold and pay such tax over to the United States Internal Revenue Service on account of such non-U.S. Member's distributive share of the Company's items of income which are subject to withholding tax pursuant to such provisions of the Code. Any amount of withholding taxes withheld and paid over by the Member Manager with respect to a Member's distributive share of the Company income shall be treated as a distribution to such Member and shall be charged against the Capital Account of such Member.[143]

8.5   Amendments for Tax Purposes. The Member Manager shall be authorized to amend this Agreement without the consent of any Member in order to attempt to ensure that the Company is not taxed as an association (or publicly traded partnership) taxable as a corporation for United States Federal income tax purposes.

8.6   Prohibited Actions. No action shall be taken by the Member Manager or any Member under this Agreement if such action would adversely affect the classification of the Company as a partnership under United States Federal income tax laws.[144]

---

[143] These taxes are merely advances on behalf of the Member and therefore are properly charged to the Capital Account of the Member.

[144] Flow-through tax treatment is fundamental for entities of this sort. Maintaining that status is one of the most important duties of the Member Manager.

ARTICLE 9
TRANSFERABILITY

9.1   Member Transfers.

(a)   A member may not[145] (voluntarily or involuntarily,
directly or indirectly) sell, exchange, assign,
transfer, convey, pledge, grant a security interest
in, mortgage, hypothecate, encumber or permit to
suffer any encumbrances on or otherwise dispose
of (other than upon a withdrawal as permitted in
this Agreement) (*Transfer*) all or any portion of
such Member's Membership Interest in the
Company or any rights, interests, or benefits with
respect thereto whether by operation of law or
otherwise unless the prior written consent of the
Member Manager shall have been obtained, which
consent may be given or withheld in the Member
Manager's sole discretion. Such Member Manager
consent shall be subject to any terms and
conditions imposed by the Member Manager. In
the event of any Transfer made in accordance
with this Agreement, the transferee shall not be
admitted to the Company as a Member without
the prior written consent of the Member Manager,
which the Member Manager may withhold in its
sole discretion, and shall be entitled only to
allocations and Distributions with respect to such
interest in the Company, and shall not have any of
the rights of a Member under the Act or this
Agreement. The interest of a transferor in the
Company shall retain the same character and be

---

[145] A blanket prohibition is required. A provision that says consent will not be
unreasonably withheld essentially makes the interest freely transferrable. That will
have both 1940 Act and Securities Act of 1933 consequences, as well as tax
consequences. For this reason, any such transfer is void. (*See* Section 9.1(e).)

subject to the same charges and allocations (including without limitation, the Management Fees and Performance Allocations) notwithstanding the Transfer thereof to a transferee.

(b)   No Member shall, without the prior written consent of the Member Manager, which the Member Manager may withhold in its sole discretion, Transfer or permit any Person holding a direct or beneficial interest in such Member, as the case may be, to Transfer a Membership Interest if (i) as a result of such Transfer, the number of security holders of the Company for purposes of the Investment Company Act shall be increased, (ii) any such Transfer, by itself or combined with other Transfers, would result in a termination of the Company under Section 708 of the Code, or (iii) any such Transfer, by itself or combined with other Transfers, would result in the Company being classified as a "publicly traded partnership" under Section 469(k) of the Code or under Section 7704 of the Code. For purposes of this Section 9.1(b), the Member Manager's determination of the number of security holders of the Company for purposes of the Investment Company Act and the Code shall be final and binding on all of the Members.

(c)   At any time after the liquidation or dissolution of a Member or following an attempted disposition by a Member of all or part of its Membership Interest not permitted under this Section 9.1, the Member Manager, at its option, may elect to require the Member, or its personal representative, heir or successor, to withdraw as a Member at the end of any calendar quarter without regard to the 5 day notice requirement of Section 4.2 hereof.

Such a withdrawal shall be subject to the provisions of Article 4 as if the Member has made a permissible withdrawal under Section 4.1.

(d)   Without the consent of any other Member, but subject to the provisions of Section 9.1(c), upon the death of a Member, the Membership Interest of the decedent Member may be transferred by will or, in the case of intestacy, by the laws of descent and distribution.

(e)   Any Transfer made other than in accordance with the terms of this Agreement (a *Void Transfer*) shall be void, and neither the Company nor the Member Manager shall be required to recognize any equitable or other claims to such interest on the part of the Transferee thereof. Any amounts otherwise distributable to a Member pursuant to Article 7, in respect of a direct or indirect interest in the Company that has been Transferred in violation of this Article 9, may be withheld by the Member Manager following the occurrence of a Void Transfer until the Void Transfer has been rescinded, whereupon the amount withheld shall be distributed without interest. An agreement or offer to sell which is by its terms conditioned upon compliance by the Transferor with the terms of this Agreement, including receiving the consent provided for in this Section 9.1, shall not be considered a Void Transfer.

9.2   Transferee Not a Member: Substituted Members. No Person acquiring an assignment or transfer of a Membership Interest (other than one Member acquiring a Membership Interest from another Member) shall become a Member except pursuant to Section 9.1 and Article 10 of this Agreement. If the consent of the Member Manager shall not have been obtained, such Transfer shall not be valid and enforceable, and such Person's interest in the Company shall be withdrawn and shall only entitle such Person to receive the Distributions and allocations of profits and losses to which the Member from which such Person received such Membership Interest would be entitled until such withdrawal occurs; and such Person shall not be entitled to any other rights granted to a Member under this Agreement. No Person may be admitted as a Member pursuant to this Article 9 or Article 10 until such Person executes this Agreement and such other documentation as required by the Member Manager, in form and substance satisfactory to the Member Manager, binding such Person to the terms and conditions of this Agreement as if such Person had been named a Member herein.

9.3   Transfer of the Manager's Interest. Subject to Section 5.17, the Member Manager may, in its sole discretion, Transfer any or all of its Membership Interest in the Company to an Affiliate of the Member Manager or the Investment Manager; provided, however, that the Member Manager shall give at least thirty (30) days prior notice to each of the other Members, which notice shall state the date as of which such Transfer is to take effect.

9.4   Transferee's Agreement to be Bound. Any Transfer of all or any part of a Member's interest in the Company (with the prior written consent of the Member Manager) shall not be effective until such transferee executes an appropriate supplement to this Agreement pursuant to which such transferee agrees to be bound by the terms and provisions of this Agreement as an assignee of the transferor's interest.

9.5   Opinions; Expenses; Other Conditions.

> (a)   Any Transfer of all or any part of an interest in the Company shall not be effective until the transferor (if the Member Manager, at its sole discretion, so requests) (i) pays the Company's expenses (including attorney's fees) in connection with such Transfer, and (ii) delivers to the Company an opinion, satisfactory in form and substance to the Member Manager, from counsel satisfactory to the Member Manager, to the effect that the transaction will not violate the Securities Act, or

any other applicable federal or state securities laws.[146]

(b)   The transferor and the transferee of the transferor's interest shall, at the request of the Member Manager, make all filings required to be made by them, respectively, with any governmental agency or other authority in connection with such Transfer, and the Member Manager is authorized to make such filings on their behalf if not timely made by them.

9.6   Transferee's Capital Account.

Any transferee shall assume the Capital Account balance (and any and all characteristics and attributes associated therewith) and all other rights or responsibilities under this Agreement of the transferor in the transferor's capacity as a Member. A transferee of the Member Manager's Membership Interest shall not be entitled to or assume any of the rights or obligations of the transferor in its capacity as the Member Manager unless such transfer is made in accordance with Sections 5.16, 5.17 or 9.3.[147]

ARTICLE 10
ADMISSION OF NEW MEMBERS

10.1   Issuance of Membership Interests; Admission of New Members.

(a)   The Member Manager, as of (i.e., immediately preceding) the start of business on the first Business Day of each calendar month or at any other time and from time to time, in its sole discretion and without any consent or action by

---

[146] Costs and expenses incurred are charged to the Member causing them.

[147] A transfer by the Member Manager made in contravention of the Agreement will not vest the executive authority of the Fund in the new Manager.

any other Member, may admit one or more Persons as new Members. Membership Interests shall be issued at a price based on the Net Asset Value of the Company determined with respect to the last Business Day immediately preceding the date of admission. There shall be no limit on the number of Membership Interests that may be so issued. The Member Manager shall have sole and absolute discretion in determining the terms and conditions with respect to any future issuance of Membership Interests provided that, any such Membership Interest shall be issued for consideration not less than the Fair Value of the Membership Interests to be issued.[148] The minimum initial Capital Contribution of a new Member shall be $1 million; except that the Member Manager may, in its sole discretion, permit any Member to make an initial Capital Contribution of less than $1 million upon such terms and conditions, if any, as the Member Manager may deem appropriate, and no Capital Contribution shall be required of any transferee, approved by the Member Manager, as a result of such Transfer; and further except, that the Member Manager may increase the minimum initial Capital Contribution for new Members to any amount greater than $1 million in its sole discretion and from time to time.

(b)   Subject to Section 5.17, the Member Manager, in its sole discretion and without any consent or action by any other Member, may admit one or more Persons as new Member Managers upon the terms and conditions as the Member Manager

---

[148] This provision allows the Manager to customize the terms and conditions of newly issued interests (voting vs. non-voting, etc.). *See* Section 10.1 (f).

may, in its sole discretion, determine, including, for the avoidance of doubt, the creation of a new class or classes of Membership Interests, including for these purposes, non-voting interests.

(c) This Agreement shall constitute the irrevocable consent of all Members to (i) the admission of Transferees as new Members, (ii) the admission of new Members or new Member Managers pursuant to this Section 10.1, (iii) the amendment of the Schedule of Members to reflect any such admissions, and (iv) all filings and other acts which the Member Manager considers necessary or appropriate to give effect to any such admissions; except that nothing in this Section 10.1(c) shall be construed to limit a Member's right to withdraw from the Company pursuant to Section 4.1.

(d) The admission of a new Member because of a Transfer shall not be a cause for the Dissolution and Termination of the Company.

(e) Each new Member shall, at the discretion of the Member Manager, be subject to a charge in such amount as the Member Manager shall require to defray the expenses incurred by or on behalf of the Company in connection with such admission.

(f) Additional Membership Interests shall be issuable from time to time in one or more classes and/or series with such designations, preferences and relative, participating, optional or other special rights, powers and duties, all as shall be fixed by the Member Manager in the exercise of its sole and absolute discretion, including, without limitation, (i) the allocation, for federal income and other tax purposes, to such series of interests of items of Company income, gain, loss, deduction and credit; (ii) the right of such class or series of Membership Interests to share in Company distributions; (iii) the rights of such class or series of Membership Interests upon Dissolution and liquidation of the Company; (iv) whether such class or series of Membership Interests are redeemable by the Company and, if so, the price at which, and the terms and conditions on which, such Membership Interests may be redeemed by the Company; (v) whether such class or series of Membership Interests is issued with the privilege of conversion and, if so, the rate at and the terms and conditions upon which such series of Membership Interests may be converted into any other series of Membership Interests; (vi) the terms and conditions of the issuance of such class or series of Membership Interests, and all other matters relating to the assignment thereof; (vii) the rights of such class or series of Membership Interests to consent on matters relating to the Company and this Agreement; and (viii) the method of calculating performance allocations to the Member Manager in respect of such class or series. The Schedule of Members shall designate the class and/or series of Membership Interest which each Member owns and the variations from the terms of this Agreement applicable to such class and/or series.

(g) Upon the issuance of any class or series of Membership Interests, the Member Manager (pursuant to the Member Manager's powers of attorney from the Members), without the approval at the time of any Member may amend any provision of this Agreement (and shall amend the Schedule of Members) and execute, swear to, acknowledge, deliver, file and record, if required, an amended Certificate of Formation and such other documents as may be required in connection therewith, as shall be necessary or desirable to reflect the authorization and issuance of such class or series of Membership Interests and the relative rights and preferences of such class or series of Membership Interests as to the matters set forth in the preceding sentence. The Member Manager is also authorized to cause the issuance of any other type of security of the Company from time to time to Members or other persons on terms and conditions established in the sole and absolute discretion of the Member Manager.

(h)   The debts, liabilities and obligations incurred, contracted for or otherwise existing solely with respect to a particular series of Membership Interests where the use of the term "series" is intended to define a segregated asset pool, shall be enforceable only against the assets and/or investments of such series and not against the assets and/or investments of the Company generally, any other series of Membership Interests thereof, or any Member Manager not associated with such series, and, none of the debts, liabilities, obligations and expenses incurred, contracted for or otherwise existing with respect to the Company generally or any other series of Membership Interests thereof shall be enforceable against the assets and/or investments of such series or a Member Manager associated with such series.

(i)   In no event shall the issuance of any series of Membership Interests adversely affect the rights and obligations hereunder of holders of any

Membership Interests or any series previously issued.[149]

ARTICLE 11
DISSOLUTION

11.1   <u>Dissolution</u>. The Company shall be dissolved and its affairs shall be wound up upon the first to occur of the following events (each, a *Liquidating Event*):

      (a)   the vote or written consent of Members who hold, in the aggregate, at least two-thirds of the Percentage Interests of all Members;

      (b)   the bankruptcy, insolvency, liquidation, termination by the Company, death, insanity, dissolution, expulsion, incapacity, retirement, resignation or withdrawal unrelated to a transfer, sale, assignment or other similar transaction of the Member Manager or the occurrence of any other event that terminates the continued membership of the Member Manager in the Company, unless within ninety (90) days after such event a "majority-in-interest" (as that term is defined in Treasury Regulations Section 301.7701-2(b)) of all of the remaining Members agree (by vote or written consent) to continue the Company and elect a new member manager. For purposes of this Agreement, bankruptcy shall mean, with respect to a Person:

---

[149] This provision is to support the ability of the parties to offer the opinion that the issuance of new interests does not materially affect the current investors.

(i) that such Person has

(1) made an assignment for the benefit of creditors;

(2) filed a voluntary petition in bankruptcy;

(3) been adjudged bankrupt or insolvent, or has had entered against such Person an order of relief in any bankruptcy or insolvency proceeding;

(4) filed a petition or an answer seeking for such Person any reorganization, arrangement, composition, readjustment, liquidation, dissolution, or similar relief under any statute, law, or regulation or has filed an answer or other pleading admitting or failing to contest the material allegations of a petition filed against such Person in any proceeding of such nature; or

(5) sought, consented to, or acquiesced in the appointment of, a trustee, receiver, or liquidator of such Person or of all or any substantial part of such Person's properties;

(ii) ninety (90) days have elapsed after the commencement of any proceeding against such Person seeking reorganization, arrangement, composition, readjustment, liquidation, dissolution, or similar relief under any statute, law, or regulation and such proceeding has not been dismissed; or

(iii)   ninety (90) days have elapsed since the appointment without such Person's consent or acquiescence of a trustee, receiver, or liquidator of such Person or of all or any substantial part of such Person's properties and such appointment has not been vacated or stayed or the appointment has not been vacated within sixty (60) days after the expiration of such stay;

(c)   the election to dissolve and terminate the Company made in writing by the Member Manager (for the avoidance of doubt, if the Member Manager elects to terminate the Company when there are outstanding Withdrawal Requests, all such Withdrawal Requests shall be deemed expunged and Termination and Dissolution shall occur under this Article 11)[150];

(d)   the time there are no Members; provided further that the personal representative of the last remaining Member or its designee or nominee shall not be admitted as a Member;

(e)   the withdrawal and retirement of all of the Member Managers as Member Managers of the Company pursuant to Section 4.6(b) where no new Member Manager has been appointed; or

---

[150] This is an innovation of the Model Agreement and is intended to avoid arguments over the priority of redemption requests. It also allows the Member Manager to act unilaterally to terminate the fund.

(f)   the entry of a decree of judicial dissolution under 6 Del. C. § 18-802.

11.2   <u>Winding Up</u>. Upon the occurrence of a Liquidating Event, the Company shall liquidate in an orderly manner as promptly as shall be practicable under the supervision and control of (a) the Member Manager[151], or (b) if there is no such Member Manager, the Person designated by a Majority in Interest of the Members (any Person designated pursuant to this Section 11.2 is herein called the *Liquidating Member*). The Member Manager or Liquidating Member, as the case may be (as liquidating trustee for the Company, the Members and all others concerned) may, in the name of, and for and on behalf of, the Company, prosecute and defend suits, whether civil, criminal or administrative, gradually settle and close the Company's business, dispose of and convey the Company's property, discharge or make reasonable provision for the Company's liabilities, and distribute to the Members any remaining assets and/or investments of the Company. The Member Manager will continue to receive the Management Fee and the Performance Allocation during the period that it is liquidating the Company.

11.3   <u>Distributions upon Dissolution</u>. Upon the occurrence of a Liquidating Event, the Member Manager or Liquidating Member, as the case may be, shall, out of Company assets and/or investments, make Distributions in the following manner and order:

(a)   To creditors, including Members who are creditors, to the extent permitted by law, in satisfaction of liabilities of the Company, whether by payment or by making of reasonable provision for payment thereof, other than liabilities for which reasonable provision for payment has been made;

---

[151] The Member Manager should be paid for its services. Whether that is at full management fee or a lesser amount is open for negotiation between the parties.

(b)   To Members and former Members in satisfaction of liabilities for Distributions under Sections 18-601 or 18-604 of the Act;

(c)   To establish such reserves[152] as the Member Manager or Liquidating Member, as the case may be, deems reasonably necessary for any contingent, foreseen or unforeseen liabilities or obligations of the Company, which reserves may be paid over by the Member Manager or Liquidating Member, as the case may be, to any attorney-at-law, or other party acceptable to the Member Manager or Liquidating Member, as the case may be, as escrow agent to be held for disbursement in payment of any such liabilities or obligations and, at the expiration of such period as shall be deemed advisable by the Member Manager or Liquidating Member, as the case may be, for distribution of the balance in the manner hereinafter provided in this Section 11.3; and

(d)   To Member Manager for any and all expenses and reimbursements due and payable as a result of winding up the Company; and

(e)   The balance, if any, to the Members pro-rata in proportion to the remaining positive Capital Account balances of such Members, as determined after taking into account all Capital Account adjustments for the Performance Year during which such liquidation occurs (other than those made pursuant to this Section 11.3(e)). Such adjustments shall include, without limitation, the Performance Allocations set forth in Sections

---

[152] These reserves include litigation reserves and indemnification obligation reserves.

7.2(c) and 4.4(a) (as applicable) for the Performance Year ending with the termination of the Company. Such amounts shall be paid by the end of the Performance Year in which such liquidation occurs (or, if later, within ninety days after the date of such liquidation).

11.4   <u>Nonrecourse to Other Members</u>. Except as provided by applicable law or as expressly provided in this Agreement, upon Dissolution of the Company, each Member shall receive a return of its Capital Contribution solely from the assets and/or investments of the Company. If the assets and/or investments of the Company remaining after the payment or discharge of the debts and liabilities of the Company are insufficient to return any Capital Contribution of any Member, such Member shall have no recourse against any other Member or the Member Manager, as the case may be.[153]

11.5   <u>Distributions in Cash or in Kind</u>.

(a)   All Distributions to a Member by the Company upon Dissolution of the Company, withdrawal or otherwise may be made in cash, Securities (which may include short positions, as well as long positions), other assets and/or investments or any combination of the foregoing, as may be selected by the Member Manager or the Liquidating Member, as the case may be, in its sole discretion. Any Distribution of any assets and/or investments in kind shall be considered a Distribution of an

---

[153] This is the key advantage of a limited liability company versus a limited partnership—the Member Manager is not liable for the obligations of the entity in the same way that a general partner is responsible.

amount equal to the assets and/or investments' Fair Value on the date of distribution.[154]

(b)   If Securities are distributed in kind, such Securities may be distributed directly to the Member or alternatively, distributed into a liquidating trust or liquidating account and sold by the Company for the benefit of the Member,[155] in which case (a) payment to such Member of that portion of his withdrawal attributable to such Securities will be delayed until such time as such Securities can be liquidated and (b) the amount otherwise due such Member will be increased or decreased to reflect the performance of such Securities through the date on which the liquidation of such Securities is effected as well s the expenses incurred to liquidate the investments and to manage the liquidating trust or liquidating account, unless other arrangements are made by the Member Manager and the Company.[156]

---

[154] It is both prudent and practical that the Fund have the ability to make distributions both in cash and in kind at its election. The proper value to be placed on assets distributed in kind is "fair value." That keeps the relative rights and burdens of the Members in balance.

[155] The Model Agreement takes a practical approach and allows assets distributed in kind to be held in a liquidating trust or escrow until sold so that cash can be distributed instead.

[156] The Model Agreement does not make provision for the payment of the expenses of the liquidating trust and liquidating account other than to indicate that any costs of the liquidation process will be deducted from the proceeds realized on sale. Of course, the parties could agree instead to have the Fund set aside cash resources to pay the costs of liquidation. It is unlikely that the Manager would be successful if it attempted to get the Members to return any amount distributed to pay expenses, so this issue needs to be provided for in the liquidating trust documents.

11.6   Certain Agreements to Continue. The exculpation provision contained in Section 5.9, the indemnification and contribution agreements contained in Section 5.8 and the agreement to keep confidential and not use certain proprietary information contained in Section 13.5 shall remain in full force and effect following the termination of the Company.[157]

11.7   Use of Company Name After Winding Up. The name "ABC Fund, LLC", and all derivations thereof belong to ABC Partners Inc. and it Affiliates. This Agreement confers on the Company a limited license only with respect to the use of the name "ABC Fund, LLC" and does not confer upon the Company or the Members any other right to the name "ABC Fund LLC," or any derivations thereof, or any name to which the name of the Company may be changed as provided in Section 2.2, or any part of any such name, or to the name of any other partnership, corporation, or other entity formed by the Company or any part of such name or names, except that the Company may use the name "ABC Fund LLC," unless the name of the Company is changed as provided in Section 2.2. Upon the termination of the Company as specified in Section 11.1, the right to use such name, and all such changed names, shall remain the property of ABC Partners Inc. and no compensation shall be paid to the Company or the Members.[158] The Company and the Members agree to take such actions as may be necessary to implement the provisions of this Section.

11.8   Termination. Upon completion of the Dissolution, winding up, liquidation, and distribution of the assets and/or investments of the Company, the Company shall be deemed terminated (the *Termination*).

---

[157] Continuation of the indemnification agreements as a matter of contract law eliminates a difficult legal issue later, namely, is an Indemnitee still indemnified for acts that occur before the termination of the Fund after termination? In other words, does the Fund have to set up a post-termination reserve? This provision makes it clear that the answer is yes.

[158] It is important that the Manager can protect his or her intellectual property, including its name and goodwill.

ARTICLE 12
VALUATION OF SECURITIES AND OTHER COMPANY ASSETS

12.1   Net Asset Value.

       (a)   The Net Asset Value of the Company will be calculated by the Accounting Agent in consultation with the Member Manager and the Investment Manager in accordance with GAAP applied on a consistent basis under the accrual basis of accounting.[159]

       (b)   The Investment Manager shall be responsible for determining the Fair Value of the assets and/or investments and liabilities in the Company[160] and in the Master Fund and the Master Fund in turn will generally provide the value of its underlying assets and/or investments on a monthly basis to each Feeder Fund, including the Company. The Investment Manager shall also make a determination if the valuation provided by the Master Fund requires further adjustment by the

---

[159] Of course, this is a reference to U.S. GAAP; for international funds, a different reference would be appropriate, perhaps to International Accounting Standards. The reference here to U.S. GAAP essentially incorporates statements of the Financial Accounting Standards Board (FASB) and other authoritative pronouncements. The use of the accrual method allows comparison on an apples-to-apples basis with other funds, in particular registered products.

[160] Because the Company can invest directly as well as through the Master Agreement, the Model Agreement has a robust Fair Value procedure intended to comply with FAS 157 and FAS 157-4.

Company because the Company holds its interest in the Master Fund as an investment. [161]

(c) If there is no Investment Manager or the Investment Manager fails in these duties in a material fashion, determined in the sole discretion of the Member Manager, the Member Manager shall undertake all valuations for all purposes of this Agreement in the place of the Investment Manager and the references herein to "Investment Manager" shall be read to refer to the Member Manager instead.[162]

(d) If the disability of the Investment Manager is removed, as determined in the sole discretion of the Member Manager, or the Investment Manager is replaced, the Member Manager can re-delegate the valuation responsibilities under this Agreement to the person or entity serving as the Investment Manager at that time, subject to the supervisory duty of the Member Manager to undertake valuations on behalf of the Company when to do so, as determined in the sole discretion of the Member Manager, is in the best interests of the Company and its Members.

---

[161] This is a common "miss"—the Master Fund is an investment of the Feeder Fund and must be treated that way in certain instances, such as where the Feeder Fund has a separate, independent business.

[162] This is a "safety valve" provision that allows the Member Manager to step in if the Investment Manager fails to perform adequately with respect to valuation matters. Note that this is intentionally separate from a termination of the Investment manager—the Investment Manager may be a good stock picker or bond manager; it may just have infrastructure issues that make it incapable of completing the valuation tasks required or maintain the proper documentation. Compliance officers for the Fund and for the Member Manager should make it a point to review valuation documentation as part of their periodic reviews.

(e)   The "Net Asset Value" or "NAV" of a Fund equals the total Fair Value of the assets and/or investments of the Fund less the total Fair Value of the liabilities of the Fund.[163]

(f)   The Net Asset Value will be calculated as of the last Business Day of each calendar month or such other day as the Member Manager, in its sole discretion, shall determine (a Measurement Date).[164]

(g)   To the extent the Company has invested in the Master Fund, the Net Asset Value of that portion of the assets of the Company is calculated based on the Company's proportionate interest in the Net Asset Value of the Master Fund. [165]

12.2   Fair Value.

The Fair Value of the investments of the Company and of the Master Fund will be reported in accordance with FASB Statement 157 (FAS 157) and FSP FAS 157-4, which establishes a framework for measuring fair value or any other method prescribed by FASB. There are several key governing principles for this process:

---

[163] The lynchpin of NAV is Fair Value. *See* Section 12.2. Note that this term has evolved from the historical "fair market value" to "Fair Value" in recognition of the fact that a good valuation for these purposes may come from a model or other source that is not reflected in a true market because one does not exist.

[164] The Measurement Date concept is used throughout the Model Agreement as the day on which various transactions occur and the NAV of the Fund is measured.

[165] In order to keep costs down and be practical wherever possible, it is anticipated that the Feeder and the Master Funds will have the same auditor. If the separate investment business of the Feeder fund develops to a point where the Fund is self-sustaining, it may be possible to have a different auditor for that line of business, or perhaps for the entire Feeder Fund itself.

(a)   The transaction to transfer an asset or liability which will form the basis of the Fair Value of an asset or liability will be deemed (by the Investment Manager) for these purposes to occur in the principal market for the asset or liability, or in the absence of a principal market, the most advantageous market for the asset or liability.[166]

(b)   The Investment Manager will not adjust the price in the principal or most advantageous market used to measure Fair Value of an asset or liability for transaction costs.[167]

(c)   The information considered and the basis for any valuation decision will be documented by the Investment Manager and the supporting data will be retained by the Investment Manager in the books and records of the Company.[168]

(d)   The Investment Manager shall determine Fair Value based on certain market participant assumptions which are referred to as inputs. Employing the present methods provided by FASB, investments will be valued according to inputs appropriate for the three level hierarchy

---

[166] *See generally*, Section 2.32 of the AICPA Investment Companies Accounting Guide. A principal market is the market with the greatest volume and level of activity for the asset or liability. The most advantageous market is the market in which the Fund would sell the asset or transfer the liability with the price that maximizes the amount that would be received for the asset or minimizes the amount that would be paid to transfer the liability.

[167] *See generally*, Section 2.33 of the AICPA Investment Companies Accounting Guide. Transaction costs are accounted for in accordance with other accounting pronouncements.

[168] *See generally*, Section 2.42 of the AICPA Investment Companies Accounting Guide.

established in FAS 157 and FSP FAS 157-4 as described below:

(i)   Level 1. Level 1[169] inputs are quoted prices (unadjusted) in active markets for identical assets or liabilities that the Master Fund or its agents have the ability to access at the Measurement Date.

(ii)   Level 2. Level 2 inputs are inputs other than quoted prices included within Level 1 that are observable for the asset or liability, either directly or indirectly. Level 2 inputs include:

(1)   Quoted prices for similar assets or liabilities in active markets;

(2)   Quoted prices for identical or similar assets or liabilities in markets that are not active (the factors described below may indicate a market is not active or that there has been a significant decrease in the volume or level of activity for the asset or liability (or similar assets or liabilities));

(3)   Inputs other than quoted prices that are observable for the asset or liability (for example, interest rates and yield curves observable at commonly quoted intervals, volatilities, prepayment speeds,

---

[169] Note that the Levels do not necessarily reflect a hierarchy where Level 1 is better than Level 2, which is better than Level 3.

loss severities, credit risks, and default rates);

(4)   Inputs that are derived principally from or corroborated by observable market data by correlation or other means (market-corroborated inputs).

(e)   Quoted Price Inputs for Level 1 and Level 2. Employing FAS 157, as amended, inputs representing quoted prices for Level 1 and Level 2 are based on the following waterfall of methods beginning with paragraph (i) below, *seriatim* until[170] an appropriate method is found:

(i)   Securities which are listed on one or more United States or non-U.S. securities exchanges (including securities which are principally traded on the Nasdaq Stock Market) shall be valued at their closing price as is customarily ascertained by the respective exchange and disseminated by quotation services such as Reuters or Bloomberg or available online.

(ii)   Securities not traded on a securities exchange or on Nasdaq, but traded in the over-the-counter market, are valued at their last reported price on the date of determination in such market as reported by a reputable source or a regulatory facility

---

[170] This begins the traditional valuation waterfall, and is used to create a simplifying assumption on what input should be checked in which order. The Investment Manager and Member Manager need to weigh in here to ensure that it is administrable and consistent with their practices.

developed to aggregate select secondary market transactions selected by the Investment Manager.

(iii)   Listed options are valued at the mean of their representative bid and asked prices on the exchange on which such options are traded on the date of determination.

(iv)   To the extent not inconsistent with the above, futures and options contracts traded on U.S. exchanges are valued at their settlement price on the exchange on which such futures or option contracts are traded on the date of determination; provided, however, that, if a futures or option contract could not be liquidated on such day due to the imposition of daily price fluctuation limits or other rules of the exchange on which such contract is traded or otherwise, the settlement price on the first subsequent day on which such contract could be liquidated will be the value of such contract for such Measurement Date.

(v)   Spot and forward contracts, futures and options contracts traded on foreign exchanges, and over-the-counter option contracts are valued by methods determined by the Investment Manager and applied on a consistent basis.

(f)   Significant Decrease in Activity. In addition, in determining Fair Value, the Investment Manager shall determine whether there has been a significant decrease in the volume and level of activity for the asset or liability when compared with normal market activity for the asset or liability (or similar assets or liabilities) by considering the following factors, among others:

(i)   Few recent transactions.

(ii)   Price quotations not based on current information.

(iii) Price quotations vary substantially over time or among market makers.

(iv)   Indices once highly correlated with Fair Value of the asset or liability are demonstrably uncorrelated with recent indications of Fair Value for that asset or liability.

(v)   Significant increase in implied liquidity risk premiums, yields, or performance indicators (such as delinquency rates or loss severities) for observed transactions or quoted prices when compared with the Investment Manager's estimate of expected cash flows, considering all available market data about credit and other nonperformance risk for the asset or liability.

(vi)   Wide bid-ask spread or significant increase in the spread.

(vii) Significant decline or absence of a market for new issuances (that is, a primary market) for the asset or liability or similar assets or liabilities.

(viii) Little publicly released information (for example, a principal-to principal market).

(g)   <u>Further Analysis of Transactions</u>. If the Investment Manager concludes there has been a significant decrease in the volume and level of activity for the asset or liability, transactions or quoted prices may not be determinative of Fair Value (for example, there may be increased instances of transactions that are not orderly). The Investment Manager will conduct further analysis of the transactions or quoted prices. The Investment Manager may make significant adjustments to the transactions or quoted prices as necessary to estimate Fair Value in accordance with FAS 157. Significant adjustments also may be necessary in other circumstances (for example, when a price for a similar asset requires significant adjustment to make it more comparable to the asset being measured or when the price is stale).

(h)   <u>Change in Valuation Techniques</u>. If there has been a significant decrease in the volume and level of activity for the asset or liability, the Investment Manager may, with respect to that investment, change the valuation techniques used or use multiple valuation techniques as appropriate (for example, the use of a market approach and a present value technique). When weighting indications of Fair Value resulting from the use of multiple valuation techniques, the Investment Manager shall consider the reasonableness of the range of Fair Value estimates, with the objective of determining the point within that range that is most representative of Fair Value under current market conditions. If the range of Fair Value estimates is very wide, the Investment Manager may do a further analysis as needed.

(i)   <u>Determination of Whether Transaction Not Orderly</u>. In determining Fair Value, the

Investment Manager shall also consider the following factors, among others, which may indicate that a transaction is not orderly:

(i)   Inadequate exposure to market prior to Measurement Date to allow for customary marketing activities.

(ii)   Customary marketing period, however seller only marketed asset or liability to one market participant.

(iii)   Seller is in or near bankruptcy (that is, distressed) or is required to sell to meet regulatory or legal requirements (that is, forced).

(iv)   Transaction price is an outlier when compared with other recent transactions.

(j)   <u>Transaction Not Orderly</u>. If the weight of evidence indicates that the transaction is not orderly, the Investment Manager shall place little, if any, weight (compared with other indications of Fair Value) on that transaction price when estimating Fair Value or market risk premium.

(k)   <u>Transaction Orderly</u>. If the weight of evidence indicates that the transaction is orderly, the Investment Manager shall consider that transaction price when estimating Fair Value or market risk premium and the weight placed on that price will depend on the volume of the transaction, the comparability of the transaction to the asset or liability being measured and the proximity of the transaction to the Measurement Date.

(l)   <u>Unable to Determine</u>. If the Investment Manager is unable to determine whether the transaction is orderly, it shall consider the transaction price when estimating Fair Value or market risk premium, however that transaction price may not be determinative and greater weight shall be placed on transactions known to be orderly.

(m)   <u>Level 3</u>. Level 3 inputs are unobservable inputs for the asset or liability.

        (i)   Unobservable inputs shall be used to measure Fair Value to the extent that observable inputs are not available, thereby allowing for situations in which there is little, if any, market activity for the asset or liability at the Measurement Date.

        (ii)   Unobservable inputs shall reflect the Investment Manager's own assumptions about the assumptions that market participants would use in pricing the asset or liability (including assumptions about risk).

        (iii)   Unobservable inputs shall be developed based on the best information available in the circumstances, which might include the Investment Manager's own data.

        (iv)   In developing unobservable inputs, the Investment Manager need not undertake all possible efforts to obtain information about market participant assumptions.

        (v)   However, the Investment Manager will not ignore information about market participant assumptions that is reasonably available without undue cost and effort. Therefore, the Investment Manager's own data used to develop unobservable inputs shall be adjusted if information is reasonably available without undue cost and effort that indicates that market participants would use different assumptions.

12.3   Special Assets and the Use of Side Pockets.[171]

The Master Fund may at times purchase, hold, transfer or otherwise dispose of Securities, assets and/or investments that are Special Assets. The Investment Manager has the right, in its absolute and sole discretion, to (a) segregate, separately account for and/or establish separate or sub-accounts (each a *Side Pocket Account*) at the Master Fund level and hold such Side Pocket Accounts in the Master Fund, or distribute interests in one or more of them *pro rata* to the shareholders of the Master Fund (including the Company, the *Shareholders*); and (b) value such assets and/or investments pursuant to the procedures set forth above.

(a)   Shareholders participating in a Special Asset will maintain the Shareholder's economic interest in the Special Asset until the sale or other disposition of such Special Asset by the Master Fund.

(b)   Should the Master Fund's assets include Special Assets, the directors of the Master Fund may compulsorily redeem a portion of the Class A, Class B and/or Class C Shares held by Shareholders and apply the proceeds towards the automatic subscription for the number of Class D Shares of the Master Fund corresponding to their

---

[171] The Model Agreement builds on lessons learned from recent market turmoil and provides a framework for the use of side pockets at both the Master Fund level and at the Feeder Fund level. Side pockets in the Master Feeder Context present special difficulties, as an asset held at the Master Fund level that has been segregated must be accounted for separately to give the allocation layers actual effect.

proportional interest in the Special Assets of the Master Fund. Class D Shares of the Master Fund may be exchanged back into Class A Shares, Class B Shares and/ or Class C Shares of the Master Fund where the Master Fund disposes of all or part of a Special Asset or otherwise determines that all or part of a Special Asset is no longer illiquid, in which case, the directors of the Master Fund shall compulsorily redeem a portion of the Class D Shares held by Shareholders and apply the proceeds towards the automatic subscription for the number of Class A Shares, Class B Shares or Class C Shares of the Master Fund corresponding to their proportional interest in the Special Asset.

(c)   Where the Master Fund has distributed interests in a Side Pocket Account to the Company, the Company may hold such interests or the Investment Manager may advise the Company to distribute some or all of such interests as a distribution directly to Members, in which case those Members shall be issued interests in a new entity formed to hold the interests in the Side Pocket Account being distributed (the *Liquidating Entity*). The Liquidating Entity shall adopt a form of governing documents equivalent to those of the Company as its governing documents and the Members shall have a proportionate interest in the Liquidating Entity equal to their proportionate Capital Account associated with the Special Asset/interests in the Side Pocket Account. If a Liquidating Entity is established, the Company shall also contribute liquid assets from the Company into the Liquidating Entity [172]in an

---

[172] Who pays for administration of a side pocket has always been a thorny issue. The Model Agreement makes clear that it is the Fund itself. This is not an administrative burden that can be or should be shifted to the Member Manager.

(continued...)

amount sufficient to pay for the costs of administration of the Liquidating Entity, as determined by the Investment Manager in its sole discretion, for a period of three years or until a liquidity event, whichever is determined by the Investment Manager, in its sole discretion, to be more likely to occur first.

(d) The Investment Manager, in its absolute and sole discretion, will determine when an investment shall be classified as a Special Asset at the Master Fund level and when it should no longer be considered a Special Asset and reintroduced as an asset available to all Shareholders. The Investment Manager may also, with respect to a Shareholder's participation in a Special Asset, restrict the Shareholder's ability to redeem its shares in the Master Fund, or place other limitations or restrictions, including receipt, release and refunding arrangements, until such investments are no longer classified as Special Assets.

(e) If the Investment Manager, in its sole discretion, has specially valued a Special Asset of the Master Fund and converted Class A, Class B and Class C Shares of the Master Fund into Class D Shares of the Master Fund, the Investment Manager shall also designate such asset as a designated investment (*Designated Investment*) at the Company level.

(continued...)

Investment losses are the responsibility of the Members, and so should the cost of winding them down.

(f)   A Member participating in a Designated Investment will maintain the Member's economic interest in the Designated Investment until the sale or other Disposition of such asset by the Master Fund and shall be considered a "Designated Investment Member" of the Company. For example, the Designated Investment Member shall receive withdrawal payments on account of such Member's remaining Capital Account without regard to the Designated Investment.

(g)   A Designated Investment Member will continue to be a Member (a *Designated Investment Member*; see Article 4 for a discussion of the consequences of remaining a Designated Investment Member) until the Designated Investment Member has received all amounts payable with respect to all Designated Investments in the Member's Designated Investment account.[173] Once the Designated Investment has been disposed of, the Designated Investment Member will receive such Member's allocable share of the proceeds from the sale, less expenses, Management Fees and Performance Allocations related to such Designated Investment. Any amounts payable to a Designated Investment Member will be paid within thirty (30)

---

[173] If the Manager and Investment Manager create a Designated Investment Account, all Members at the time of creation remain members of the Designated Investment Account until there is a liquidity event. Note: The Investment Manager can avoid these procedures by simply choosing to Fair Value all securities, including those that are difficult to value. To minimize liability, however, many choose not to do so, and instead red circle these investments. In the limited partnership context, these side pockets can merely be special allocations. However, that device is not possible in the corporate context (the case where the Master Fund is an offshore entity taxed as a corporation for U.S. federal income tax purposes).

days following the total Disposition of the Designated Investment, at which point the Net Asset Value of the Company attributable to the Designated Investment sold should be known.

12.4   No Liability. In no event and under no circumstances shall the Member Manager, the Investment Manager or the Company's administrator incur any individual liability or responsibility for any determination made or other action taken or omitted by them in good faith in attempting to value the assets of the Company and the Company shall hold them harmless with respect to their actions taken in good faith in the application of this policy.

12.5   Investment Manager's Determination Binding.

The Investment Manager's determination of the Fair Value of Securities and property held by the Company shall be final and binding on the Company and the Members.[174]

12.6   NAV Expressed in Dollars.

The Net Asset Value of the Company will be expressed in dollars, and the value of any assets and/or investments or liabilities expressed in terms of currencies other than dollars will be translated into dollars at the prevailing market rates as determined by the Investment Manager.

12.7   Suspension.

The determination of the value of the assets and/or investments of the Company may be suspended when and if withdrawals are ever suspended.

---

[174] The Investment Manager's and the Member Manager's sensitivity over valuation issues is palpable through the Model Agreement. The valuation decisions made in real time are not subject to second-guessing, and the parties agree that such valuations are final and binding.

ARTICLE 13
GENERAL PROVISIONS

13.1   <u>Notices and Consents</u>. Any notice, demand, or other communication required or permitted to be given pursuant to this Agreement shall be in writing, or by electronic mail if authorized and requested by the Member, and shall have been sufficiently given for all purposes if

(a)   delivered personally to the Member,

(b)   delivered to a recognized overnight courier service for next day delivery to the Member at such Member's address appearing on the books and records of the Company, unless such Member shall have filed with the Company a written request that notices intended for such Member be delivered to another address, in which case the notice shall be at the address designated in such request, or

(c)   sent by registered or certified mail, postage prepaid, addressed to the Member at its address specified above, or

(d)   if sent by electronic transmission to the Member at the Member's last known address for electronic delivery as recorded with the Company. Except as otherwise provided in this Agreement, any such notice, demand, or communication shall be deemed to be effective on the date personally delivered to the Member, or one business day after delivery to the courier service, or three business days after the date on which it was deposited in a regularly maintained receptacle for the deposit of United States mail, addressed and sent as set forth in this Section 13.1, or upon transmission if sent by electronic mail. All consents required or permitted hereunder shall be in writing, or by electronic mail delivered to the Member Manager, the Administrator or other party that may be designed by the Member Manager, provided such electronic communications has been requested and authorized by the Member.[175]

13.2   Entire Agreement. This Agreement and the Certificate of Formation contain the entire agreement among the Members with respect to the subject matter hereof, and supersede all prior agreements and understandings, written or oral, among the parties with respect hereto and thereto, whether or not relied or acted upon.[176] No course of conduct pursued or acquiesced in, and no oral agreement or representation

---

[175] Electronic commerce and signatures require consent. The Model Agreement's companion Subscription Agreement (not reproduced here) contains a consent to electronic records and communications and to the use of electronic signatures.

[176] This is a standard "merger clause" for an agreement of this sort. However, it takes on added significance in light of the fact that this is not the only document handed to investors who considering making an investment. Other documents given to investors include the Subscription Agreement and the private placement memorandum. In our Model Document set, the signature page to the Subscription Agreement and Operating Agreement is combined—the Subscription Agreement acts to modify the Operating Agreement to the extent of any inconsistencies. The private placement memorandum and any other offering materials (such as pitch books, PowerPoint presentations, and tear sheets) that are incorporated into the private placement memorandum are, and should be, mere disclosure documents, describing the business and legal "deal" among the parties. To the extent they are inconsistent, the contract (i.e., the operating agreement) must control, except where either a case of detrimental reliance can be made out by an investor, or a regulator imposes detrimental reliance through its regulatory review/enforcement function. The best case, of course, is to make certain that, at all times, the offering materials are consistent with the operating agreement. It is for this reason that the investment strategy and style limitations should not be contained in or appended to the operating agreement, nor should key personnel be listed in the operating agreement. The operating agreement provides the legal and operational framework for the fund. Modifications to disclosure documents and offering materials must always be vetted against the operating agreement before first use. For this reason, among others, best practices dictate that marketing personnel should not have control over the content of offering materials.

subsequently made by the Members, and no usage of trade, shall amend this Agreement, or impair or otherwise affect any Member's obligation, rights, and remedies pursuant to this Agreement.

13.3   Amendments; Other Actions of Member Manager.

(a)   Any provision to the contrary contained herein notwithstanding, the Member Manager may, without the consent or approval of any Member, make any and all amendments to this Agreement which will be binding on the Members, which such amendments include, but are not limited to, those necessary to:

(i)   to add to the representations, duties or obligations of the Member Manager,

(ii)   to reflect any change of information contained in the Schedule of Members hereto in accordance with the Agreement;

(iii)   to correct a typographical error, correct any manifest error, correct or supplement any provision which may be inconsistent with any other provision;

(iv)   to delete from or add to any provision required to be so deleted or added by a federal or state securities commission or regulator (including without limitation, the Securities and Exchange Commission, Commodity Futures Trading Association and Financial Industry Regulatory Authority), which addition or deletion is deemed by such commission for the benefit of or protection of the Members;

(v)   provided, however, that no amendment shall be adopted pursuant to this Section

13.3 unless the adoption thereof does not affect the status of the Company as a partnership for Federal income tax purposes; and

(vi) further provided that in the event the amendment would materially and adversely affect any Member, the "negative consent"[177] of the affected Member, or if more than one Member is materially and adversely affected thereby, the "negative consent" of the affected class or series of Members, will be required, such consent being evidenced by the "negative consent" of the affected Member, or if applicable, of the majority of the class or series of Members (measured by Percentage Interest) materially and adversely affected by such change; and further provided that "negative consent" shall mean consent by the required Member or Members evidenced by either affirmative consent or the failure to respond (or object) within the time specified by the Member Manager.

(b) The Member Manager shall send each Member a copy of any amendment adopted pursuant to this Section 13.3.

(c) Upon the adoption of any amendment to this Agreement, the amendment shall be executed by the Member Manager and all of the Members and, if required, shall be recorded in the proper records

---

[177] The Manager can modify the Agreement unless such amendment would have a material adverse effect. The procedures opt for a negative consent procedure for most matters; *see also* Section 13.3(e).

of each jurisdiction in which recordation is necessary for the Company to conduct business or to preserve the limited liability of the Members. Any such adopted amendment may be executed by the Member Manager on behalf of the Members pursuant to the power of attorney granted herein.

(d) In the event this Agreement shall be amended pursuant to this Section 13.3, the Member Manager shall amend the Certificate of Formation of the Company to reflect such change if such amendment is required or if the Member Manager deems such amendment to be desirable and shall make any other filings or publications required or desirable to reflect such amendment, including, without limitation, any required filing for recordation of any certificate or other instrument or similar document of the type contemplated by this Agreement.

(e) Every matter submitted for a vote or consent of the Members shall be determined by the affirmative vote or consent of Members holding in the aggregate a majority by Net Asset Value of the Company attributable to the Capital Accounts, except as otherwise provided herein or required by the Act.

13.4   <u>Reports to Members</u>. The Member Manager shall cause to be prepared and mailed to each Member audited annual financial statements within 120 days after the end of each Fiscal Year, and quarterly unaudited performance reports within sixty days after the end of the first three calendar quarters.[178] All results will be reported in United States dollars in compliance with GAAP.

13.5 _Proprietary Information_. Notwithstanding anything to the contrary contained in this Agreement, the method of operation of the Member Manager and its investment strategies and selections are confidential and proprietary to the Member Manager. For the period that this Agreement remains in effect and for a period of two years thereafter, each Member agrees for himself and his successors and assigns (i) always to keep secret and confidential all such information and (ii) never to use, or permit the use of, any such information in any fashion for his personal benefit or the benefit of any third Person. The Member Manager shall be entitled to equitable relief in the event of any violation, threatened or actual, by any Member, and each Member agrees that money damages are not an adequate remedy for any such violation.

13.6 _Arbitration_.

(a)   It is understood and agreed between the parties hereto that any and all claims, grievances, demands, controversies, causes of action or disputes, of any nature whatsoever (including, but not limited to, tort and contract claims, and claims upon any law, statute, order or regulation) (hereinafter _Disputes_), arising out of, in connection with, or in relation to (i) this Agreement, or (ii) questions of arbitrability under this Agreement, shall be resolved by final, binding, nonjudicial arbitration [179]in accordance with the Federal

---

[178] This is to comply with the custody rules of the SEC. The Manager must make certain that the accountants hired can meet this deadline.

[179] All disputes under the Agreement are subject to binding arbitration. This may or may not save costs and may or may not be beneficial to the Fund. Professional arbitrators are more likely to understand how the industry operates, but there are no guarantees that that works for or against the Member Manager, the Investment Manager, or the Fund. An alternative approach would be to require alternative

(continued...)

Arbitration Act, 9 U.S.C. Section 1, <u>et seq.</u> pursuant to the following:

(i)   Any party may send another party written notice identifying the matter in Dispute and invoking the procedures of this Section (the *Dispute Notice*). Within fourteen (14) days after delivery of the Dispute Notice, the parties involved in the Dispute shall meet at a mutually agreed upon location in Wilmington, Delaware for the purpose of determining whether they can resolve the Dispute themselves by written agreement, and, if not, whether they can agree upon an impartial third party arbitrator (the *Arbitrator*) to whom to submit the matter in Dispute for final and binding arbitration.

(ii)   If such parties fail to resolve the Dispute, by written agreement, or agree on the Arbitrator within the later of fourteen (14) days after any such initial meeting, or within thirty (30) days from the delivery of the Dispute Notice, any such party may make written application to the Judicial Arbitration and Mediation Services (*JAMS*), in Wilmington, Delaware for the appointment of a single Arbitrator to resolve the Dispute by arbitration. At the request of JAMS, the parties involved in the Dispute shall meet with JAMS at its offices within ten (10) calendar days of such

(continued...)

dispute resolution but allow unresolved matters to go to the courts if necessary. Still a third way is to allow all disputes to go to court.

request to discuss the Dispute and the qualifications and experience that each party respectively believes the Arbitrator should have; provided, however, that the selection of the Arbitrator shall be the exclusive decision of JAMS and shall be made within thirty (30) days of the written application to JAMS.

(iii)   Within thirty (30) days of the selection of the Arbitrator, the parties involved in the Dispute shall meet in Wilmington, Delaware with such Arbitrator at a place and time designated by such Arbitrator after consultation with the parties and present their respective positions on the Dispute. Each party shall have no longer than one (1) day to present its position, the entire proceedings before the Arbitrator shall be no more than three (3) consecutive days, and the decision of the Arbitrator shall be made in writing no more than thirty (30) days following the end of the proceeding. Such an award shall be a final and binding determination of the Dispute and shall be fully enforceable as an arbitration decision in any court having jurisdiction and venue over such parties. The prevailing party (as determined by the Arbitrator) shall in addition be awarded by the Arbitrator such party's own legal fees and expenses in connection with such proceeding. The non-prevailing party (as determined by the Arbitrator) shall pay the Arbitrator's fees and expenses.

(b)   By signing this Agreement, the parties hereto are giving up their respective rights to a jury trial.

(c)   Notwithstanding anything to the contrary herein, the parties agree to generally use their commercially reasonable, good faith efforts to resolve any disagreement with respect to the operation of this Agreement prior to seeking a claim or other relief under this Section 13.6.

13.7   Special Powers of Attorney.[180]

(a)   Each Member hereby irrevocably makes, constitutes and appoints the Member Manager, with full power of substitution, the true and lawful representative and attorney-in-fact of, and in the name, place and stead of such Member, with the power from time to time to make, execute, sign, acknowledge, swear to, verify, deliver, record, file and/or publish:

(i)   this Agreement or any amendment to this Agreement adopted in accordance with the provisions of this Agreement;

(ii)   the Certificate of Formation and any amendment thereof required because this Agreement is amended, including, without limitation, an amendment to effectuate any change in the membership of the Company or in the Capital Contributions of the Members;

(iii)   any application, certificate, certification, report or similar instrument or document required to be submitted by or on behalf of

---

[180] This provision allows the Member Manager to execute documents that have otherwise been approved under the procedures in the agreement without the necessity of having to go to investors to obtain their manual or electronic signatures.

the Company to any governmental or administrative agency or body, to any exchange, board of trade, clearing corporation or association or similar institution or to any self-regulatory organization or trade association; and

(iv)   all such other instruments, documents and certificates which, in the opinion of legal counsel retained by the Member Manager, may from time to time be required by the laws of the United States of America, the State of Delaware or any other state or foreign jurisdiction in which the Company shall determine to do business, or any political subdivision or agency thereof, or which such legal counsel may deem necessary or appropriate to effectuate, implement and continue the valid and subsisting existence and business of the Company as a limited liability company.

(b)   Each Member is aware that the terms of this Agreement permit certain amendments to this Agreement to be effected and certain other actions to be taken or omitted by or with respect to the Company without his or its consent. If an amendment of the Certificate of Formation or this Agreement or any action by or with respect to the Company is taken by the Member Manager in the manner contemplated by this Agreement, each Member agrees that, notwithstanding any objection which such Member may assert with respect to such action, the special attorneys specified above are authorized and empowered, with full power of substitution, to exercise the authority granted above in any manner which may be necessary or appropriate to permit such amendment to be made or action lawfully taken or omitted.

(c)   Each Member is fully aware that each Member will rely on the effectiveness of this special power-of-attorney with a view to the orderly administration of the affairs of the Company.

(d)   This power-of-attorney is a special power-of-attorney and is coupled with an interest in favor of the Member Manager and as such (x) shall be irrevocable and continue in full force and effect notwithstanding the subsequent death or incapacity of any party granting this power-of-attorney, regardless of whether the Company or the Member Manager shall have had notice thereof; (y) may be exercised for a Member by a facsimile signature of the Member Manager or, after listing all of the Members, including such Member, by a single signature of the Member Manager acting as attorney-in-fact for all of them; and (z) shall survive the delivery of an assignment by a Member of the whole or any portion of his or its interest in the Company, except that where the assignee thereof has been approved by the Member Manager for admission to the Company as a new Member, this power-of-attorney given by the assignor shall survive the delivery of such assignment for the sole purpose of enabling the Member Manager to execute, acknowledge, and file any instrument necessary to effect such admission.

13.8   Insurance. The Member Manager may cause the Company to purchase and maintain, at the expense of the Company,[181] insurance on

---

[181] This provision allows the Fund to purchase insurance to backstop the indemnification and other obligations of the Fund, at the Fund's expense. It also

(continued...)

behalf of the Member Manager or any agent appointed by the Member Manager against any liability asserted against it or him or incurred by it or him in any such capacity or arising out of its or his status as such, whether or not the Company would have the power to indemnify it or him against such liability under the provisions of Section 5.8.

13.9   Benefit Plans.

(a)   The Company shall not knowingly engage in any transaction with respect to a Benefit Plan Member that would result in a violation of ERISA or of the prohibited transaction provisions of the Code by the Company, the Member Manager, or such Benefit Plan Member. The Company and the Member Manager may rely on any representation made by a Member as to any matter subject to ERISA or §4975 of the Code and shall be fully protected in so relying. Any such Member shall indemnify and hold harmless the Member Manager and the Company for any liability or costs whatsoever resulting from such Member's representation.

(b)   Department of Labor Regulation 29 C.F.R. §2510.3-101, as modified by section 3(42) of ERISA, provides that, subject to certain exceptions, a Benefit Plan that acquires an equity interest in an entity that is neither a publicly-offered security nor a security issued by a registered investment company will be deemed to have acquired an undivided interest in each of the underlying assets of the entity (*Plan Assets*),

---

(continued...)

allows for the purchase of a retrospective reporting endorsement (tail) to fund the Fund's obligations under Section 11.6.

thereby subjecting (a) any Person who exercises authority or control over or provides investment advice with respect to the assets of the entity to fiduciary liability with respect to the Benefit Plan and (b) subjecting the investments and other transactions of the entity to the prohibited transaction rules of ERISA and the Code. If the Company's assets become "Plan Assets," the Member Manager will take appropriate steps so that the Member Manager and the Company will comply with all the applicable provisions of ERISA and the Code, or in the alternative, redeem such Member's interest in the Company in the Member Manager's sole discretion.

13.10   Information Regarding Members and Accounts. The Member Manager shall provide to any Member [182]information regarding Members or accounts requested by such Member subject to the following:

(a)   Information regarding Members and accounts may be inspected upon the reasonable written demand of any Member to the Member Manager or its duly authorized representative, during regular business hours for any purpose reasonably related to such Member's interest as a Member.

(b)   The Member Manager shall establish reasonable standards governing, without limitation, the information and documents to be furnished and the time and the location, if appropriate, of furnishing such information and documents. Costs of providing such information and

---

[182] It is often suggested that the Fund should not be obligated to deliver information to Members who threaten suit. It is doubtful whether an embargo like that would survive a subpoena, and so no such limitation is included in the Model Agreement.

documents shall be borne by the requesting Member. The Company shall be entitled to reimbursement for it's direct, out-of-pocket expenses incurred in declining unreasonable requests (in whole or in part) for information or documents.

(c)   The Member Manager may keep confidential from Members for such period of time as it deems reasonable any information that it reasonably believes to be in the nature of trade secrets or other information that the Member Manager, in good faith believes would not be in the best interests of the Company to disclose or that could damage the Company or its business or that the Company is required by law or by agreement with a third party to keep confidential.

13.11   Headings[183]. The headings in this Agreement are for convenience of reference only, and shall not be used to interpret or construe any provision of this Agreement.

13.12   Waiver. [184] No failure of a Member to exercise, and no delay by a Member in exercising, any right or remedy under this Agreement shall constitute a waiver of such right or remedy. No waiver by a Member of any such right or remedy under this Agreement shall be effective unless made in a writing duly executed by all Members.

---

[183] Sections 13.12 and 13.16 are often derisively referred to as "boilerplate." Nothing can be further from the truth. *See* notes below.

[184] Non-waiver is an important reservation of rights, as normal commercial activity invariably requires accommodations to "get things done." If a waiver in one instance effected a modification of the agreement from thence forth, that would chill the exercise of that flexibility. Such modifications to procedures are "one-offs," and this ensures that that is the case.

13.13   Severability.[185] Whenever possible, each provision of this Agreement shall be interpreted in such a manner as to be effective and valid under applicable law. If any provision of this Agreement shall be prohibited by or invalid under such law, it shall be deemed modified to conform to the minimum requirements of such law, or if for any reason it is not deemed so modified, it shall be prohibited or invalid only to the extent of such prohibition or invalidity without the remainder thereof or any other such provision being prohibited or invalid.

13.14   Binding.[186] This Agreement shall be binding upon, and inure to the benefit of, all Members and each of the permitted successors and assignees of the Members.

13.15   Counterparts. [187] This Agreement may be executed in counterparts, each of which shall be deemed an original instrument and all of which shall constitute one and the same agreement.

13.16   Governing Law. [188] This Agreement shall be governed by, and interpreted and construed in accordance with, the internal laws of the State of Delaware, without regard to its principles of conflict of laws.

---

[185] The same with severability. Judges need instructions on when and if a defective provision (in the court's view) can be excised or whether an entire agreement must be scrapped. This provision gives the judge the instruction he or she needs from the agreement of the parties.

[186] This is an expression of consideration—each party tenders its agreement to be bound along with cash or property (from the investor) and an interest in the Fund (from the Fund) as the other good and valuable consideration to support the enforceability of the agreement.

[187] This provision allows signatures to appear on different pieces of paper—when all of the copies are assembled, they form one document.

[188] Governing law should mirror the law under which the Fund was formed. The last clause—"without regard to its principles of conflict of laws"—means that a court or arbitrator would not have to go to Delaware's conflict of laws jurisprudence to see if it would direct the parties back to the state where the Manager is or where the Investment Manager is, or where the officers of the Fund

(continued...)

IN WITNESS WHEREOF, the parties hereto have duly executed this Agreement as of the date so indicated.

ABC PARTNERS INC., as Member Manager

By:_____
    Ms ABC, President

[The signature pages for the Members other than the Member Manager are on record with the Company]

(continued...)

(if any) are, or where the investor is. Rather, a court or arbitrator can simply apply Delaware substantive law.

Appendix A:
Fund Formation Questionnaire

FUND STRUCTURE	
Fund Name:	_____
Choice of Entity:	☐ Limited Partnership ☐ LLC
Jurisdiction/State of Formation:	☐ Delaware ☐ Other _____
Parallel Offshore Fund:	☐ N/A ☐ Yes ☐ No
Address of Principal Place of Business:	_____ _____ _____
Name and Address of General Partner or Managing Member:	_____ _____ _____
Name and Address of Investment Adviser:	_____ _____ _____
Registration of the General Partner: (If an LP)	The General Partner is: ☐ a federally registered investment adviser ☐ registered as an investment adviser in the state of _____ ☐ Not registered as an investment adviser in any state or with the SEC (Contact Pepper Hamilton).

Registration of the Investment Adviser	The Investment Adviser is: ☐ a federally registered investment adviser ☐ registered as an investment adviser in the state of _____ ☐ Not registered as an investment adviser in any state or with the SEC (contact Pepper Hamilton).
Relationship between General Partner and Investment Adviser	_____ _____ _____
Affiliations of General Partner or Managing Member:	_____ _____ _____
Investment Company Act of 1940 Considerations – Investment Company Exemption:	☐ 3(c)(1) – 100 Beneficial Owners* *Must be Qualified Clients if a Performance Fee is paid ☐ 3(c)(7) – Qualified Purchasers
Estimated Assets in the Fund:	$_____
Proposed Launch Date:	_____
If escrow is used, what bank acts as escrow agent	_____ _____ _____
Who receives interest earned by Escrowed Funds – The Investor or the Fund	_____ _____ _____

FUND ECONOMICS	
Management Fee:	_____% Payable: ☐　In Arrears ☐　In Advance (contact Pepper Hamilton) ☐　Monthly ☐　Quarterly
Performance Allocation (including method of calculation and clawbacks, if any):	_____ _____ _____
High Water Mark and Method and Frequency of Calculation:	_____ _____ _____
Organizational Expenses Cap for the Fund:	*The Fund will bear $_____ or ALL (circle if applicable/cross out if not applicable)* The Management Company or General Partner will bear the excess. ☐　Yes ☐　No
Amortization of Organizational Expenses:	☐　Yes ☐　No If yes, specify the period over which organizational expenses will be amortized and whether your accountants have consented. [Note – GAAP requires immediate expensing; tax rules have specially applicable limits] _____
Partnership Expenses	_____

INVESTMENT OBJECTIVE, STRATEGIES AND LIMITATIONS

Investment Objective **:	 (Attach additional sheets if necessary.)
Investment Style**:	❏ Direct Investment in Securities ❏ Fund-of-Funds ** *Please attach a narrative of the management philosophy or methodology for the Fund. If the Fund is a fund-of-funds, describe how underlying hedge funds and managers are selected.*
Investment Strategies and Limitations (*please describe all investment strategies and investment limitations of the Fund*):	❏ Equity Securities ❏ Short sales ❏ Letter and control stock ❏ Commodities, commodities futures contracts, commodities options ❏ Financial futures ❏ Options purchases and writings ❏ Real estate ❏ Other investment companies ❏ Foreign securities ❏ New Issues (F/K/A "Hot" Issues) ❏ Other: _____
Margin and Borrowing:	In trading securities, the Fund ❏ may ❏ may not Borrow or trade on margin.
Diversification Requirements:	❏ None ❏ Asset _____

	❑ Long/Short _____
	❑ Issuer _____
	❑ Industry/Sector _____

RISKS AND CONFLICT OF INTEREST CONSIDERATIONS
(check all that apply)

Inherent Risks of an Investment in the Fund **:	❑ Limited Operating History
	❑ Dependence on Management
	❑ Performance Allocation
	❑ Diversification
	❑ Market Risks
	❑ Liquidity Risks
	❑ Other
	_____
	** *Please describe the risks that are inherent to the investment adviser's investment style and the securities in which the Fund may invest.*

Conflicts of Interest **:	❐ Management services to other funds, whether competing or not
	❐ Investments and loans to affiliates
	❐ Joint investments
	❐ Transactions with general partner, management company or principals
	Specify: _____
	❐ Indirect compensation to principals
	❐ Soft dollars
	❐ Other:
	_____
	❐ Acts as Adviser or Subadviser to ERISA accounts
	❐ Acts as Adviser or Subadviser to "Plan Assets"
	❐ Acts as Adviser or Subadviser to "a '40 Act Registered Fund" (contact Pepper Hamilton)
	** *Please describe any actual or potential conflicts of interest among the Fund, the principals, the general partner, the management company and the Fund's investors. In addition, please describe how conflicts of interest will be managed.*

CONTRIBUTIONS AND WITHDRAWALS

Contributions by the Principals:	The Principals will invest (directly or indirectly) on an aggregate basis $_____ in the Fund. This investment
	❐ Is mandatory
	❐ Is not mandatory
Minimum Investment of Investors:	$_____
	Authority to Waive Minimum by General Partner or Managing Member
	❐ Yes

	❏ No
Timing and Frequency of Capital Contributions	❏ Monthly ❏ Quarterly ❏ Annually
Withdrawal Restrictions	Frequency: ❏ Monthly ❏ Quarterly ❏ Annually ❏ Lock-Up Period of _____ ❏ Withdrawals are subject to _____ days prior written notice ❏ Withdrawals are subject to a withdrawal fee of _____% ❏ Minimum amount of withdrawal: $_____ ❏ Amount which must be left in capital account in the event of a partial withdrawal: $_____
Liquidity Issues on Withdrawals:	_____ _____
Contributions and Withdrawals In-Kind	❏ Yes ❏ No
DISTRIBUTION AND INVESTOR PROFILE	
Offering	❏ Public Offering ❏ Private Placement of Securities – Regulation D Offering ❏ Offshore targeted offering
Investor Profile	❏ High Net Worth Individuals

	☐ Pension Plans (i.e. ERISA) • If checked, are the investment adviser and General Partner ERISA bonded? _____ • If checked, are the investment adviser and General Partner Qualified Plan Asset Managers? _____ ☐ Trusts ☐ Other Private Investment Funds ☐ Other: _____

Investor Suitability Requirements:	✓ Accredited Investor ☐ Qualified Client (as defined under the Investment Advisers Act of 1940) ☐ Qualified Purchaser ☐ Other Suitability Requirements: _____
Blue Sky:	Please list the states in which interests in the Fund will be offered: _____ _____ _____ Note: NY requires PRE registration before any offering is undertaken.
Placement Agents:	☐ Yes (Please list by name and indicate whether a signed agreement is in place.) _____ _____ _____ ☐ No
Distribution of	☐ Hard Copies

Memorandum and Subscription Materials:	☐ Electronic delivery and commerce. Note: unless specifically declined, a consent to electronic records, communication and signatures will be included in the document package – or -- ☐ Decline electronic commerce
ADMINISTRATIVE AND GOVERNANCE MATTERS	
Powers of General Partner or Managing Member:	_____ _____ Note: Standard provisions will be listed unless Modification is noted.
Multiple General Partners or Managing Members:	_____ _____ If there are multiple general partners or managing members, please describe how management decisions be made (i.e. by unanimous consent or simple majority vote).
Management or Other Special Committees:	_____ _____ Describe management committees, their members, and powers.
Undertakings Regarding Taxes – will the fund make tax distributions to enable investors to have the cash to pay taxes? Note – the usual answer is NO.	☐ Yes ☐ No _____ _____
Amendments to Partnership/Operating Agreement	_____ _____

	Note: Standard provisions will be listed unless Modification is noted.
Provisions and Causes for Dissolution of the Fund	_____ _____ Note: Standard provisions will be listed unless Modification is noted.
Periodic Audits and Reports to Investors	_____ _____ Note: Standard provisions will be listed unless Modification is noted.
Valuation of Assets and Frequency of Valuation (include means for fair price valuation and transparency):	_____ _____ Note: Standard provisions will be listed unless Modification is noted.
Fiscal Year of The Fund:	❑ June 30 (contact Pepper Hamilton) ❑ December 31
Auditor:	_____ _____
Administrator:	_____ _____
Custodian and Custody Arrangements:	_____ _____